BUSINESS BUZZWORDS TO BURY YOUR SOUL

THE DEFINITIVE DICTIONARY OF CORPORATE NONSENSE

N. RON PONZI

CLEVELAND STEAMER PRESS

INTRODUCTION TO THE MADNESS

Welcome, daring corporate linguist, to the grand colosseum of gibberish otherwise known as *Business Buzzwords to Bury Your Soul: The Definitive Dictionary of Corporate Nonsense*. You've just snagged a hotwired pass into the mental madhouse where "synergy" breakdances with "mission critical" on the conference room table and "value-add" masquerades as a philanthropic unicorn in a cheap wig.

Peek inside these pages and watch as "helicopter managers" hover like caffeinated dragonflies over your thinning patience, "chainsaw consultants" hack through your comfort zones, and "moonshot divisions" shoot for greatness but land in a crater of PowerPoint slides. This is your linguistic landfill, your conference call dystopia, where every "band-aid solution" peels back to reveal seething chaos. Don't believe the "blue sky thinking" hype—these buzzwords are more like radioactive fog, seeping into your neurons until you start believing that "boiling the ocean" is a legit action item.

But fear not, intrepid reader. After flipping through *Business Buzzwords to Bury Your Soul*, you will be the one "facipulating" the narrative. You'll call out "bullshit bingo" like a seasoned ringmaster and refuse to "marinate" another half-baked directive. Soon you'll deploy your newfound lexicon to "triangulate" flimsy strategies and "drill down" on faux-inspirational slogans until the suits who utter them develop a sudden case of "analysis paralysis."

Armed with this "definitive dictionary of corporate nonsense," you'll no longer "synergize" when you mean "agree" or "circle back" when you mean "ignore." You'll laugh at the "silo mentality" and rip apart "greenfield site" daydreams with a knowing grin. Thanks to this compendium, empty phrases will become piñatas of pomposity for you to smash apart at will. You've learned their language; now it's time to conquer it.

So go forth, oh jargon Jedi. Let your new vocabulary gleam like a neon shiv through the darkness of empty corporate chatter. Unmask the "core competencies" that never existed, juke past the "value proposition" so vague it might be a low-rent horoscope, and revel in the chaos as "unicorn" startups prance nervously before your withering stare.

Welcome to the front lines of linguistic liberation. After devouring these definitions, you'll blast through boardrooms like a witty wrecking ball, toppling towers of trite terminology. By the last page, you won't just survive the semantic swamp—you'll emerge as its supreme overlord, sipping mock-lattes while the hollow buzz of "mission-critical deliverables" withers in the fluorescent gloom.

This is *Business Buzzwords to Bury Your Soul: The Definitive Dictionary of Corporate Nonsense*. Enjoy your stay. Just don't forget to circle back once you've had your fill of corporate Kool-Aid—there's always another "game changer" waiting in the wings, desperate for a seat at the conference table of absurdity.

10 GREAT WAYS TO USE BUSINESS BUZZWORDS TO BURY YOUR SOUL

Wielding the The Definitive Dictionary of Corporate Nonsense

1. **Perform Ninja-Level Sarcasm Attacks**: When the VP babbles about "greenfield initiatives," casually flip to the definition and hold the book open with a silent, knowing smirk—like you're revealing top-secret files on their misguided "value proposition."

2. **Whisper Jargon to Confuse Mediocrity**: During a "mission critical" meeting that feels like slow-motion "analysis paralysis," lean over to a coworker and murmur, "Aces in their places..." They'll spend the rest of the day pondering what cryptic prophecy you've just unleashed.

3. **Brandish Like a Magical Shield in Huddles**: In those impromptu "huddle sessions" that produce nothing but "vicious agreement," hold this dictionary up and pretend to consult it, then shake your head solemnly. Let the frantic nodders wonder which page has exposed them.

4. **Trigger Ironic Enlightenment at Presentations**: When a keynote speaker drones on about "A/B testing" and "synergy," thumb through the pages with theatrical flair. At the Q&A, fake surprise: "Oh, sorry, I was just verifying if that's *really* innovative."

5. **Silent Mic Drops to 'Focus on Results' Fans**: Each time a manager howls "Focus on results!" like a wounded banshee, flip open to the "80/20" entry and politely point. Let them know you're hip to their hollow priorities. Bonus: do it slowly for maximum passive-aggressive zen.

6. **Subtle Shadiness for Shady Deals**: If someone crows about how "above-board" their project is, just open the page for "above-board," make a show of reading it, then raise an eyebrow. No words needed—just pure, concentrated side-eye.

7. **Unmask Faux-'Consensus Building'**: During a deadlocked meeting where everyone pretends to agree, grab the dictionary, read "consensus building" out loud, and watch them scramble like corporate roaches exposed to fluorescent honesty.

8. **Dodge Donkey Work Like a Pro**: When asked to chase "low-hanging fruit" (aka do extra busywork), point to the definition of "low-hanging fruit" and smirk. Consider adding a whispered "hard pass" for good measure.

9. **Nuke Bragging About 'Retaining Talent'**: If HR crows about retention strategies, find "churn" and nonchalantly show it to them. Smile as their boasts evaporate faster than "philanthropy" in a budget meeting.

10. **Preempt Agile Banter Before a Big Pitch**: Just before someone says "We'll be agile," flip to "agile," give a conspiratorial wink, and close the book quietly. Let them know you hold the whole deck of corporate-lingo cards, and you're not afraid to play them.

Use these tactics wisely, and you'll transform each word from a weapon of empty bluster into a pin to pop their office-speak balloon. With this dictionary, you're the gatekeeper of unvarnished truth—no "deep dives" required.

THE NUMBERS
ARE FOR 1031 EXCHANGE BECAUSE TURNING TAXES INTO TEMPORARY TRIVIA TAKES TENACITY—TRUST THOSE NUMBERS AND KEEP UNCLE SAM AT BAY

1031 EXCHANGE

n. A U.S. tax provision allowing an investor to sell a property and reinvest the proceeds in a similar property while deferring capital gains tax.

Commonly employed by real estate investors seeking tax efficiency.

"Larry insisted on doing a 1031 exchange, because apparently turning tax liability into the government's problem is his idea of savvy investing."

Related Terms: Cap rate, Investment property, Real estate closing, REIT (Real Estate Investment Trust)

2.0

n. A term indicating a newer, supposedly improved version of something.

Commonly employed by marketers and product teams to rebrand or refresh existing offerings.

"Our boss called the rebranded memo 'Memo 2.0,' because nothing screams innovation like tacking on a number and calling it a day."

Related Terms: Business transformation, Digital transformation, Innovation

30,000-FEET VIEW

n. A high-level perspective emphasizing overall strategy rather than details.

Commonly employed by executives and managers when avoiding specifics or encouraging big-picture thinking.

"Karen gave us the 30,000-feet view of the project, which was super useful if you prefer vague optimism over actual details."

Related Terms: 360-degree view, Across the piece, High level

360-DEGREE VIEW

n. A comprehensive perspective that considers all aspects or angles of a situation.

Commonly employed by leaders and consultants to imply thorough understanding.

"When the CEO demanded a '360-degree view' of the problem, we all pretended our heads weren't spinning in circles already."

Related Terms: 30,000-feet view, Holistic approach, Break down silos

501(C)(3)

n. A U.S. tax code designation for nonprofit organizations that are tax-exempt due to charitable, religious, or educational purposes.

Commonly employed by nonprofits and donors seeking tax benefits and credibility.

"After registering as a 501(c)(3), the charity proudly announced it could now spend donations on a building fund instead of, you know, charity work."

Related Terms: Nonprofit sector, Nonprofit compliance, Nonprofit governance, Charitable giving

80/20

n. The Pareto Principle, stating that roughly 80% of results come from 20% of causes.

Commonly employed by strategists, managers, and efficiency experts to focus on the most impactful factors.

"If the 80/20 rule is correct, then 80% of the nonsense we hear in meetings comes from the same 20% of people—looking at you, Steve."

Related Terms: Low-hanging fruit, Lean methodology, Cost-benefit analysis

A
IS FOR ACTION BECAUSE ACCELERATING ACHIEVEMENTS AVOIDS AIMLESS ADMINISTRIVIA —ALWAYS ACT, DON'T JUST ARGUE.

A/B TESTING

n. Comparing two versions of something (like an ad or webpage) to see which performs better with an audience. Commonly employed by marketing and UX teams to optimize conversion rates and engagement.

"We ran an A/B test on the newsletter subject lines and learned that people prefer edgy sarcasm over heartfelt sincerity—who knew?"

Related Terms: Conversion rate, User experience (UX), Data-driven decisions

ALAP (AS LATE AS POSSIBLE)

abbr. + adj. Meeting a deadline as late as possible without missing it. Commonly employed by procrastinators and teams juggling multiple deadlines.

"My mantra is ALAP, because who wants to deliver early and ruin the suspense?"

Related Terms: ASAP (As Soon As Possible), Just-in-case inventory

AML (ANTI-MONEY LAUNDERING)

abbr. + n. Procedures and regulations designed to prevent financial crimes like money laundering. Commonly employed by banks, financial institutions, and compliance officers.

"The AML checks made Rick feel like a VIP villain from a Bond movie, minus the cool accent and a secret volcano lair."

Related Terms: KYC (Know Your Customer), Regulatory compliance

AP (ACCOUNTS PAYABLE)

n. The money a company owes to its suppliers or vendors. Commonly employed by finance and accounting departments managing outgoing payments.

"Our AP department sends out checks so late I'm convinced they're trying to see if the suppliers will forget we owe them money."

Related Terms: AR (Accounts Receivable)

AR (ACCOUNTS RECEIVABLE)

n. The money owed to a company by its customers. Commonly employed by finance and accounting teams to track incoming payments.

"When I see AR, I think, 'Great, more IOUs from customers who act like paying bills is a charming hobby they've yet to pick up.'"

Related Terms: AP (Accounts Payable), Churn

AR (AUGMENTED REALITY)

n. Technology overlaying digital content onto the physical world. Commonly employed by product developers, marketers, and sales teams to enhance product demos or customer experiences.

"Using AR, the sales team pretended our outdated products were futuristic marvels, as if holograms could distract from actual defects."

Related Terms: VR (Virtual Reality), Innovation

ASAP (AS SOON AS POSSIBLE)

abbr. Indicating urgency and priority in completing a task. Commonly employed by managers and coworkers when they need something done yesterday.

"'ASAP' in our office means 'We needed it yesterday, but didn't bother telling you until today. Good luck!'"

Related Terms: ALAP (As Late As Possible), FOMO (Fear Of Missing Out)

ABOVE MY PAYGRADE

phrase. Tasks or responsibilities considered beyond one's assigned authority or expertise. Commonly employed by employees to dodge taking on strategic or executive-level decisions.

"Deciding the company's global expansion strategy is definitely above my paygrade, but hey, I'll pretend to know everything anyway."

Related Terms: Aces in their places, HiPPO (Highest-Paid Person's Opinion)

ABOVE-BOARD

adj. Truthful, honest, and straightforward in actions or communication. Commonly employed by leaders and auditors emphasizing ethical conduct.

"The CFO assured us everything was above-board, which is code for 'I'll lie to your face with impeccable posture.'"

Related Terms: Transparency, Due diligence

ACCELERATOR

n. A program offering startups mentorship, resources, and sometimes funding to speed growth. Commonly employed by entrepreneurs and early-stage companies seeking rapid development.

"Our startup joined an accelerator, because who wouldn't trade a chunk of equity for free stale coffee and a mentor who's never heard of weekends?"

Related Terms: Incubator, Seed round, VC (Venture Capital)

ACCOUNTABLE CARE ORGANIZATION (ACO)

n. A healthcare model where a network of providers shares responsibility for patient outcomes and costs. Commonly employed by healthcare administrators and insurers to improve care quality and efficiency.

"The ACO promised better patient outcomes, or at least a few less lawsuits involving misplaced test results."

Related Terms: Bundled payments, Value-based care

ACES IN THEIR PLACES

phrase. Assigning the most qualified individuals to roles best suited to their strengths. Commonly employed by managers and HR when trying to optimize team performance.

"If we actually put aces in their places, half our management team would be out looking for jobs with less creative job titles."

Related Terms: Above my paygrade, Culture fit

ACLUISTIC

adj. Completely clueless. Commonly employed by anyone describing a person who remains oblivious despite multiple explanations.

"After the fifth explanation, Tina remained acluistic about the concept of profit margins, blinking like a deer in headlights."

Related Terms: Mushroom management, Meanderthal, Bubble mentality

ACROSS THE PIECE

phrase. Affecting or influencing an entire project, team, or organization, rather than a single part. Commonly employed by executives making changes that impact everyone.

"The CEO announced changes that would apply across the piece, as if throwing buzzwords at us could hide the coming chaos."

Related Terms: 30,000-feet view, 360-degree view, Holistic approach

ACTION

n. An initiative or step taken toward achieving a goal. Commonly employed by managers, project leads, and team members who finally want something to happen.

"We decided to take action after six months of PowerPoint marathons—who knew doing something could help?"

Related Terms: Action item, Bias for action, Take this offline

ACTION ITEM

n. A specific, assigned task that comes out of a meeting or discussion. Commonly employed by project managers, team leads, and note-takers desperate for productivity.

"Our weekly meeting ended with exactly one action item: stop having so many useless meetings."

Related Terms: Agenda, Deliverable, Tasked

ACTIONABLE

adj. Providing enough clarity and detail to be acted upon immediately. Commonly employed by consultants, executives, and anyone allergic to vague suggestions.

"The CEO demanded actionable insights, so we added bullet points and pretended complexity was optional."

Related Terms: Action item, Key takeaway, Flesh out

AD CAMPAIGN

n. A coordinated series of advertisements sharing a common theme or message. Commonly employed by marketers, advertisers, and brands aiming to burn cash in style.

"Our ad campaign tried evoking nostalgia, but the only memory customers had was ignoring us."

Related Terms: Ad creatives, Cross-channel marketing, A/B testing

AD CREATIVES

n. The visual, textual, or multimedia content of an advertisement. Commonly employed by design teams, marketing agencies, and creatives who think stock photos are art.

"Our ad creatives featured dancing toasters—apparently, that's how we sell cloud software now."

Related Terms: Ad campaign, CMP (Creative Management Platform), Value add

AD EXCHANGE

n. A digital marketplace where publishers and advertisers buy and sell ad inventory programmatically. Commonly employed by digital marketers, ad tech companies, and algorithms trying to match eyeballs with slogans.

"We hit the ad exchange hoping for premium slots, but ended up next to clickbait about alien diets."

Related Terms: RTB (Real-Time Bidding), Programmatic advertising, Ad inventory

AD FRAUD

n. Deceptive activities generating fake ad impressions or clicks, wasting budgets. Commonly employed (unwillingly) by advertisers, and eagerly by scammers feeding on naive campaigns.

"Our CFO sobbed when we discovered ad fraud turned our 'viral' reach into bot clicks from a haunted server farm."

Related Terms: Ad viewability, CPM (Cost-per-impression), Programmatic advertising

AD INVENTORY

n. The amount of advertising space a publisher has available to sell. Commonly employed by publishers, media buyers, and anyone treating websites like billboard farms.

"We had so much ad inventory our homepage looked like Times Square and Las Vegas had a flashy baby."

Related Terms: Ad exchange, Ad network, Supply-side platform (SSP)

AD INVENTORY MANAGEMENT

n. The process of organizing, pricing, and optimizing available ad space. Commonly employed by publishers, media managers, and ad ops teams juggling virtual billboards.

"Our ad inventory management strategy: guess a price and hope advertisers don't laugh too hard."

Related Terms: <u>Ad inventory</u>, <u>Programmatic advertising</u>, <u>DSP (Demand-side platform)</u>

AD NETWORK

n. A company that connects advertisers with websites or apps hosting ads, often pre-programmatic. Commonly employed by advertisers, publishers, and old-school media buyers remembering the pre-RTB era.

"We used an ad network to fill our ad slots, effectively subcontracting our confusion to a third party."

Related Terms: <u>Ad exchange</u>, <u>Programmatic advertising</u>, <u>Ad targeting</u>

AD RETARGETING

n. Showing ads to users who previously interacted with a brand or visited a website. Commonly employed by marketers, advertisers, and stalker-like algorithms refusing to be forgotten.

"After one visit to a cat bed page, ad retargeting haunted my feeds with furry cushions at 3 AM—purr-fect."

Related Terms: <u>Behavioral targeting</u>, <u>Cookie tracking</u>, <u>Conversion rate</u>

AD ROTATION

n. The practice of cycling different ads in the same placement to test performance or prevent fatigue. Commonly employed by advertisers, ad ops teams, and A/B testers who can't pick a favorite banner.

"Our ad rotation meant viewers saw everything from dancing bananas to whispering staplers before unsubscribing."

Related Terms: <u>A/B testing</u>, <u>Ad server</u>, <u>Ad creatives</u>

AD SERVER

n. A technology platform delivering ads to websites or apps, tracking performance and targeting. Commonly employed by publishers, advertisers, and agencies deploying ad campaigns programmatically.

"We blamed the ad server for our weird banner placements, because blaming software is cheaper than hiring talent."

Related Terms: <u>Ad inventory</u>, <u>Ad rotation</u>, <u>Viewability</u>

AD TARGETING

n. Selecting specific audiences for ads based on demographics, behavior, or context. Commonly employed by marketers, advertisers, and data wizards playing matchmaker between products and eyeballs.

"Our ad targeting got so narrow we ended up showing car ads only to left-handed baristas named Chad."

Related Terms: Behavioral targeting, Contextual targeting, Conversion rate

AD VIEWABILITY

n. A metric ensuring an ad is actually seen by a user, not just served. Commonly employed by advertisers, publishers, and quality controllers preventing "invisible" impressions.

"Our ad viewability improved once we stopped placing banners below the 'scroll-to-boredom' line."

Related Terms: Ad fraud, Viewability, Programmatic advertising

ADD SOME COLOR

phrase. To provide additional detail or context to clarify a situation. Commonly employed by managers, colleagues, and presenters when vague summaries need a splash of explanation.

"The CFO said, 'Add some color to these numbers,' so I drew a rainbow chart—apparently not what he meant."

Related Terms: Flesh out, Context, Marinate

ADD VALUE

phrase. To enhance the worth or usefulness of something, typically a product, service, or discussion. Commonly employed by managers, advisors, and teammates pushing for more meaningful contributions.

"We tried to add value by including free stickers—customers remained sticker-neutral at best."

Related Terms: Value proposition, Value add, Bring it to the table

ADDRESS

v. To deal with or tackle an issue, problem, or question directly. Commonly employed by managers, leaders, and facilitators turning complaints into actionable steps.

"The VP said we'd address the complaints—so we formed a taskforce to study how to form a taskforce."

Related Terms: Action item, Marinate, Drill down

ADHOCRACY

n. An organizational philosophy favoring flexible, adaptive structures over rigid hierarchies. Commonly employed by innovators, startups, and chaos enthusiasts who think org charts are suggestions.

"In our adhocracy, we traded titles for nicknames and strategies for 'just winging it.'"

Related Terms: Agile, Skunkworks (or Skunk Works Project), Disruption

ADJOURN

v. To end a meeting or session officially. Commonly employed by chairs, facilitators, and grateful attendees escaping endless discussions.

"We adjourned the meeting after concluding that we have no conclusion—progress?"

Related Terms: Agenda, Action item, Take this offline

ADJUSTABLE-RATE MORTGAGE (ARM)

n. A mortgage with an interest rate that changes periodically based on market conditions. Commonly employed by homebuyers, lenders, and financial advisors rolling the dice on rate fluctuations.

"Our ARM felt like a financial roller coaster—exciting until we realized we hate roller coasters."

Related Terms: Fixed-rate mortgage, Foreclosure, Equity

ADMIN

n. Short for "administration" or "administrator," referring to roles managing operations or providing support. Commonly employed by HR, office managers, and teams needing paperwork to magically file itself.

"Our admin scheduled so many meetings I suspected a secret plot to measure our pain threshold."

Related Terms: Administrivia, HR (Human Resources), Backseat driver

ADMINISTRIVIA

n. Trivial administrative tasks consuming time but adding little strategic value. Commonly employed by employees, managers, and interns drowning in pointless forms.

"We spent the morning on administrivia—filing folders and printing memos no one will read."

Related Terms: Busy work, Donkey work, Paper

ADOPTION PROCESS

n. The steps taken by users, customers, or employees to embrace a new product, service, or policy. Commonly employed by product managers, change agents, and marketers tracking who's jumping on the bandwagon.

"Our adoption process was so smooth that users barely noticed we had replaced their favorite button with a llama icon."

Related Terms: Customer journey, Buy-in, Transitioning

ADVOCACY

n. Public support or recommendation of a particular cause, policy, or idea. Commonly employed by nonprofits, activists, and thought leaders trying to move needles and warm hearts.

"Our advocacy efforts included heartfelt pleas and leaflets—turns out everyone's allergic to leaflets."

Related Terms: Policy advocacy, Community outreach, Philanthropy

AFFILIATE MARKETING

n. A marketing arrangement rewarding affiliates for each visitor or customer brought by their own marketing efforts. Commonly employed by bloggers, influencers, and companies capitalizing on fans hawking their wares.

"Our affiliate marketing plan had random strangers pitching our product—surprisingly better than our in-house team."

Related Terms: Influencer marketing, User acquisition, Conversion rate

AFFORDABLE CARE ACT (ACA)

n. A U.S. healthcare reform law aiming to provide affordable health insurance and reduce costs. Commonly employed by policymakers, healthcare administrators, and insurers wrestling with mandates.

"The ACA changed how we think about coverage—now we think about paperwork and forms more often."

Related Terms: 501(c)(3), Value-based care, ACO (Accountable care organization)

AFFORDABLE HOUSING

n. Housing made available at prices accessible to lower- or middle-income households. Commonly employed by urban planners, policymakers, and nonprofits seeking homes for everyone.

"Affordable housing in our city means an apartment so small you can microwave dinner from your bed."

Related Terms: Zoning laws, Subsidized housing, Community outreach

AGENDA

n. A list of items to be discussed in a meeting, ideally preventing aimless rambling.

Commonly employed by meeting hosts, project managers, and attendees clinging to structure.

"Our agenda included 'Intro,' 'Discussion,' and 'Despair,' because we plan efficiently around here."

Related Terms: Action item, Adjourn, Take this offline

AGGRESSIVE MEDIOCRITY

n. Pursuing average results with stubborn intensity, refusing excellence or improvement. Commonly employed humorously by employees and critics describing organizations aiming for "good enough" with gusto.

"Our team's aggressive mediocrity ensured we hit every target halfway—truly consistent underachievement."

Related Terms: Mediocrity, BAU (Business-as-usual) trap, Status quo bias

AGILE

adj. A methodology or mindset favoring iterative development, frequent feedback, and quick responses to change. Commonly employed by software teams, product managers, and anyone allergic to year-long roadmaps carved in stone.

"We embraced Agile so thoroughly that we sprinted right into another sprint, never pausing to breathe."

Related Terms: Adhocracy, Iterate, Lean methodology

AGREEANCE

n. A nonstandard term for agreement, used informally or mistakenly. Commonly employed by colleagues who think "agreeance" sounds fancy, but HR gently recommends "agreement."

"We reached agreeance that we should stop saying agreeance—ironic harmony achieved."

Related Terms: Consensus building, Vicious agreement, Buy-in

AHA MOMENT

n. A sudden realization or insight that clarifies a problem or sparks an idea. Commonly employed by creatives, innovators, and employees after too many coffee refills.

"Our aha moment occurred when we realized customers don't want more features, just fewer errors."

Related Terms: A/B testing, Deep dive, Brain dump

AIR IT OUT

phrase. To openly discuss issues, concerns, or grievances to clear the air. Commonly employed by team leads, facilitators, and therapists disguised as coworkers.

"We decided to air it out about the broken printer—turns out everyone hated it, including the printer."

Related Terms: Chime in, Circle back, Facipulate

AL DESKO

adv. Eating at one's desk, often due to overwork or a grim acceptance of reality. Commonly employed by stressed employees, workaholics, and interns who dare not leave their post.

"Our al desko lunches were so routine we debated installing a kitchen chair under the desk."

Related Terms: Time-poor, Hostage mentality, Busy work

ALIGN UPON

phrase. To agree on a shared direction or decision. Commonly employed by managers, execs, and anyone who finds "agree" too simple.

"We must align upon our next steps, said the boss, as we collectively rolled our eyes in alignment."

Related Terms: Alignment, Consensus building, Buy-in

ALIGNMENT

n. The state of being in agreement or harmony with goals, values, or directions. Commonly employed by leaders, strategists, and HR insisting unity matters.

"We achieved alignment on the project's vision after a 3-hour meeting—apparently, nodding counts as agreement."

Related Terms: Align upon, Vision, Marinate

ALL HAT, NO CATTLE

phrase. Someone who talks big but lacks substance or action, referencing Texas ranchers. Commonly employed by critics, coworkers, and witty southerners calling out empty bravado.

"Our VP boasted about innovation, but shipped nothing—classic all hat, no cattle scenario."

Related Terms: Empty suit, Mickey Mouse, Corporate lingo

ALTRUISM

n. Selfless concern for the well-being of others. Commonly employed by nonprofits, philanthropists, and HR departments framing mandatory volunteering.

"Our company's altruism ended at T-shirt donations, because apparently generosity stops at cotton blends."

Related Terms: Philanthropy, Mission-driven, Social enterprise

ANALYSIS PARALYSIS

n. Overthinking decisions so extensively that no action is taken. Commonly employed by strategists, data nerds, and anyone who loves spreadsheets more than outcomes.

"Our analysis paralysis meant we studied our failures so thoroughly we forgot to fix them."

Related Terms: Deep dive, Marinate, Perfection paralysis

ANALYTICS

n. The systematic use of data and statistics to glean insights and inform decisions. Commonly employed by data scientists, marketers, and leaders who love pie charts.

"Our analytics showed people clicking everywhere except 'Buy Now,' a digital scavenger hunt for revenue."

Related Terms: Machine Learning, Benchmarking, Conversion rate

ANGEL INVESTOR

n. An individual who invests personal funds into a startup, often early and high-risk. Commonly employed by entrepreneurs, founders, and dreamers hoping rich strangers like their napkin sketches.

"Our angel investor wrote a check after hearing our pitch—hope he doesn't notice it's scribbled in crayon."

Related Terms: VC (Venture Capital), Unicorn, Bootstrapping

ANNUAL GIVING

n. Yearly donations or contributions to nonprofits or institutions. Commonly employed by fundraisers, development officers, and donors with seasonal guilt.

"Our annual giving campaign tried emotional pleas, but donors responded better to free keychains."

Related Terms: Fundraising campaign, Donor stewardship, 501(c)(3)

APOLOGIES

n. Expressions of regret or remorse for mistakes or wrongdoing. Commonly employed by PR teams, managers, and anyone caught with their hand in the cookie jar.

"We issued apologies so generic they could fit any scandal—scalable humility at its finest."

Related Terms: Whistleblower protection, CYA (Cover Your Ass), Donor recognition

APPRAISAL

n. The assessment or evaluation of value, performance, or quality. Commonly employed by HR (for performance reviews), real estate agents, and CFOs pricing everything.

"Our employee appraisal concluded that Bob excels at existing—so he got a neutral shrug rating."

Related Terms: Benchmark, Bequest, Due diligence

ARTIFICIAL INTELLIGENCE (AI)

n. Computer systems simulating human intelligence, learning from data and improving over time. Commonly employed by data scientists, tech giants, and anyone hoping robots solve their problems.

"Our AI recommended selling umbrellas in the desert, proving it's still 'learning.'"

Related Terms: Machine Learning, Deep learning, Disruption

AT CAPACITY

phrase. Operating at full load with no room for additional tasks, resources, or people. Commonly employed by managers, employees, and IT admins explaining why nothing more can fit.

"We're at capacity, so adding another project is like pouring coffee into an already overflowing mug."

Related Terms: Zero cycles, Time-poor, Busy work

AT THE END OF THE DAY

phrase. A cliché indicating a final conclusion or the bottom-line point after all considerations. Commonly employed by managers, execs, and colleagues wrapping up rambles with a final zinger.

"At the end of the day, we realized we could've said this in one sentence—yesterday."

Related Terms: In the loop, Going forward, It is what it is

AT THE HELM

phrase. In a position of leadership or control. Commonly employed by boards, managers, and reporters describing who's steering the corporate ship.

"With our new CEO at the helm, we're charting a course for maybe-not-crashing-this-time seas."

Related Terms: At capacity, Judicial independence, At the end of the day

ATTRIBUTION MODELING

n. Determining which marketing channels or touchpoints deserve credit for a conversion. Commonly employed by digital marketers, analysts, and anyone trying to justify ad budgets.

"Our attribution modeling suggested our 'Unicorn GIF' campaign deserved all the credit — magical indeed."

Related Terms: Analytics, Conversion rate, Behavioral targeting

B

IS FOR BOOTSTRAPPING
BECAUSE BURNING THROUGH
BARRELS OF BORROWED BUCKS
IS FOR BABIES—BETTER TO
BUILD YOUR BUSINESS ON YOUR
OWN BUDGET.

B2B (BUSINESS TO BUSINESS)

abbr. Business-to-Business, referring to transactions between companies rather than individual consumers. Commonly employed by marketers, sales teams, and enterprises selling software to other enterprises.

"We do B2B (Business to Business) sales, meaning we sell boredom in bulk to other corporations."

Related Terms: B2B, B2C (Business to Consumer), Market analysis

B2C (BUSINESS TO CONSUMER)

abbr. Business-to-Consumer, referring to transactions directly between businesses and individual consumers. Commonly employed by retailers, DTC brands, and marketers crafting irresistible 10% off codes.

"Our B2C approach: pretend every customer is a best friend who loves coupons and emojis."

Related Terms: B2B, Customer journey, Conversion rate

BAU (BUSINESS AS USUAL)

abbr. Business As Usual, standard operations without change or innovation. Commonly employed by managers, employees, and critics lamenting static routines.

"Our BAU meant repeatedly painting the Titanic's deck chairs while ignoring the iceberg."

Related Terms: Business-as-usual (BAU) trap, Stagnation, Status quo bias

BOMA (BUILDING OWNERS AND MANAGERS ASSOCIATION)

n. A professional organization for commercial real estate professionals, providing standards and advocacy. Commonly employed by property managers, developers, and anyone worshiping the code of vacant offices.

"Joining BOMA meant learning that building codes have codes of their own—joy."

Related Terms: Building code, Property management, Zoning laws

BACK BURNER (TWO-WORD VERSION)

phrase. To temporarily deprioritize or postpone action on a task or project. Commonly employed by managers, team leads, and procrastinators who've run out of sticky notes.

"We put that initiative on the back burner, where half-finished ideas simmer into tepid regret."

Related Terms: Put on the backburner, Marinate, Circle back

BACKBURNER (AS A STANDALONE TERM)

n. A metaphorical place where postponed tasks or ideas linger until rediscovered or forgotten. Commonly employed by colleagues, managers, and deadlines that don't mind dust.

"Our backburner overflowed with dreams deferred—at least we had a buffet of stale concepts."

Related Terms: Back burner, Marinate, Don't boil the ocean

BACKBURNER/FRONTBURNER

n. A comparison indicating which tasks are less (backburner) or more (frontburner) prioritized. Commonly employed by managers, project leads, and chefs metaphorically sorting priorities.

"Our backburner/frontburner chart resembled a stove of chaos—no one knew what to cook first."

Related Terms: Back burner, Marinate

BACKSEAT DRIVER

n. Someone who attempts to control or dictate actions without having authority or responsibility. Commonly employed by teammates, coworkers, and critics of unsolicited "advice."

"Our backseat driver boss gave instructions from afar, never touching the wheel but judging the route."

Related Terms: Micromanagement, Helicopter manager, Facipulate

BAIT AND SWITCH

n. A deceptive marketing tactic where a promoted product is unavailable and a more expensive substitute is offered. Commonly employed by dubious sales teams, shady retailers, and anyone thinking honesty is overrated.

"Our promo promised cheap laptops, but after customers arrived, we pulled a bait and switch with pricey monitors."

Related Terms: Ad fraud, Blame game, Pork-barrel project

BALL IN [SOMEONE'S] COURT

phrase. Indicating it's another person's turn or responsibility to take action. Commonly employed by managers, negotiators, and friends tired of doing all the work.

"After sending the proposal, the ball was in the client's court—where it collected dust and regret."

Related Terms: Action item, Buy-in, Take this offline

BAND-AID SOLUTION

n. A quick, temporary fix that doesn't address the root cause. Commonly employed by rushed managers, panicked teams, and anyone hoping problems vanish on their own.

"Our band-aid solution stopped the leak for a day, then the flood returned with interest."

Related Terms: Flogging a dead horse, Mickey Mouse, Donkey work

BANDWIDTH

n. The capacity, either time, attention, or resources, that one has to handle additional tasks. Commonly employed by employees, managers, and IT folks explaining why they can't take more on.

"I have zero bandwidth for another meeting—my brain's traffic jammed like rush hour."

Related Terms: At capacity, Zero cycles, Busy work

BANNER AD

n. A graphical advertisement displayed on a webpage, often at the top or side. Commonly employed by advertisers, publishers, and designers who wish 'click me!' was a personality.

"Our banner ad promised excitement, but users treated it like wallpaper—unseen and unclicked."

Related Terms: Ad creatives, Ad viewability, Programmatic advertising

BARKING ORDERS

phrase. Giving directives loudly and aggressively, often without explanation. Commonly employed by overbearing bosses, stressed managers, or anyone channeling a drill sergeant.

"The VP kept barking orders until we formed a choir of nods and muffled sighs."

Related Terms: Micromanagement, Helicopter manager, Facipulate

BATCH AND QUEUE

n. A processing method where work is grouped (batched) and then processed in sequence (queued). Commonly employed by manufacturing lines, IT operations, and anyone not a fan of real-time anything.

"Our batch and queue system turned simple tasks into a waiting line worthy of theme parks."

Related Terms: Lean methodology, Bottleneck, Workflow

BEAN COUNTER

n. A derogatory term for accountants or finance staff seen as focusing solely on numbers. Commonly employed by frustrated creatives, managers, and anyone who wants bigger budgets.

"The bean counter refused to fund our 'idea lab'—apparently dreams don't have ROI."

Related Terms: Fiscal responsibility, Penny wise, pound foolish, Benchmarking

BEHAVIORAL RETARGETING

n. Showing ads to users based on their previous behaviors, such as browsing history or site interactions. Commonly employed by advertisers, marketers, and algorithms that remember your 3 AM window shopping.

"Behavioral retargeting meant after I glanced at a blender once, kitchen gadget ads followed me like a needy puppy."

Related Terms: Ad retargeting, Behavioral targeting, Cookie tracking

BEHAVIORAL SEGMENTATION

n. Dividing customers into groups based on their behaviors, like purchase history or usage patterns. Commonly employed by marketers, analysts, and product teams profiling customers like a Netflix thriller.

"Our behavioral segmentation revealed that 10% of users love cat memes, and the other 90% tolerate them."

Related Terms: Behavioral targeting, Lookalike audience, Analytics

BEHAVIORAL TARGETING

n. Delivering ads or content to users based on their past actions and interests. Commonly employed by marketers, advertisers, and data wizards who know too much about your late-night searches.

"*Our behavioral targeting aimed at coffee lovers at midnight—proving we feed insomnia for profit.*"

Related Terms: Ad targeting, Ad retargeting, Contextual targeting

BELLWETHER

n. An indicator or predictor of future trends. Commonly employed by analysts, investors, and forecasters treating certain data points as crystal balls.

"*Our top client's sudden exit was a bellwether for a coming stampede out the door.*"

Related Terms: Canary in the coal mine, Benchmark, Key takeaway

BENCHMARK

n. A standard or point of reference against which things can be compared or assessed. Commonly employed by analysts, project managers, and anyone needing a yardstick in a hazy world.

"*We set a benchmark, then missed it, then lowered it—goalposts on wheels at their finest.*"

Related Terms: Benchmarking, Appraisal, Analytics

BENCHMARKING

n. Comparing processes or performance metrics to industry standards or best practices. Commonly employed by consultants, analysts, and leaders wanting to confirm everyone else struggles too.

"*Our benchmarking revealed we're slightly less awful than the competition—champagne all around!*"

Related Terms: Benchmark, Best practices, Analytics

BEQUEST

n. A gift or donation made through a will, often to nonprofits or institutions. Commonly employed by development officers, donors, and lawyers ensuring the future is funded.

"*Our bequest included antique vases—terrific, now we're a charity with fancy dust collectors.*"

Related Terms: Endowment fund, Annual giving, Philanthropy

BEST PRACTICE

n. A method or approach widely accepted as superior because it consistently yields desirable results. Commonly employed by managers, consultants, and HR training modules championing "gold standards."

We compiled all our best practices into a 200-page manual everyone promptly ignored."

Related Terms: Benchmarking, Core competencies, Key takeaway

BIAS FOR ACTION

n. A tendency to take decisive steps quickly rather than overanalyzing. Commonly employed by leaders, entrepreneurs, and restless teams who think spreadsheets are for wimps.

"Our bias for action meant we jumped off the cliff first, then wondered if we had a parachute."

Related Terms: Actionable, Agile, Marinate

BIG PICTURE

n. The overall perspective or main idea, ignoring minor details. Commonly employed by executives, strategists, and managers who see forests, not trees.

"Our CEO gave us the big picture—unfortunately, no one drew the details to reach it."

Related Terms: 30,000-feet view, Vision, In the weeds

BIPARTISAN SUPPORT

n. Agreement or cooperation between two political parties typically opposed to each other. Commonly employed by policymakers, lobbyists, and dreamers who believe unity can happen.

"Securing bipartisan support was like herding cats that hate each other's taste in catnip."

Related Terms: Policy advocacy, Public policy, Consensus building

BITE THE BULLET

phrase. To endure a painful or unpleasant situation that can't be avoided. Commonly employed by employees, managers, and anyone facing tough decisions sans anesthesia.

"We decided to bite the bullet and tell the client our product is basically a fancy doorstop."

Related Terms: [Bite the bullet is somewhat standalone], At the end of the day, Boil the ocean (contrast complexity)

BLAME GAME

n. The practice of assigning fault rather than solving problems. Commonly employed by dysfunctional teams, political campaigns, and toddlers with cookies.

"Our meeting devolved into a blame game so fast we considered awarding points."

Related Terms: Burning bridges, Shifting the blame, Playing politics

BLEEDING EDGE

adj. Referring to technology or ideas so advanced they're risky and unproven. Commonly employed by innovators, early adopters, and marketing hype machines wearing jetpacks.

"Our bleeding edge AI predicted pizza preferences, but only succeeded in confusing hungry customers."

Related Terms: Disruption, Cutthroat, Blockchain

BLESSING

n. Approval or endorsement to proceed, often from someone in authority. Commonly employed by managers, executives, and boards making "go/no-go" decisions sound holy.

"We got the CFO's blessing to spend money, a rare miracle worthy of a corporate choir."

Related Terms: Buy-in, Good catch, Executive decision

BLOCKCHAIN

n. A decentralized digital ledger of transactions spread across a network of computers. Commonly employed by crypto enthusiasts, fintech startups, and hype merchants promising transparency.

"Our blockchain solution stored data so securely even we couldn't figure it out."

Related Terms: Blockchain technology, Blockchain-based solutions, DeFi (Decentralized Finance)

BLOCKCHAIN TECHNOLOGY

n. The underlying tech enabling blockchain's secure, tamper-proof records. Commonly employed by developers, investors, and consultants throwing buzzwords like confetti.

"With blockchain technology, we promised no middlemen—just 10 new middle-layers of code."

Related Terms: Blockchain, Cryptocurrency wallet (Crypto wallet), Smart contracts

BLOCKCHAIN-BASED SOLUTIONS

n. Applications or services built on blockchain technology, promising transparency and trust. Commonly employed by startups, consultancies, and investors hoping it's not just a fad.

"Our blockchain-based solution tracked coffee beans from farm to cup, impressing nobody but the CTO."

Related Terms: Blockchain, Blockchain technology, Disruption

BLOCKING AND TACKLING

n. A metaphor from American football meaning handling the basic, essential tasks. Commonly employed by managers, project leads, and coaches who think sports analogies solve everything.

"Before we try VR marketing, let's do some blocking and tackling—like updating our broken contact forms."

Related Terms: Backseat driver, Donkey work, Core competencies

BLUE SKY THINKING

n. Creative, unconstrained brainstorming that ignores practical limitations. Commonly employed by strategists, innovators, and HR trainers desperate for "visionaries."

"Our blue sky thinking session ended with a plan to sell 'shoes for fish'—untethered indeed."

Related Terms: Big picture, Think outside the box, Marinate

BOARD OF DIRECTORS

n. A group of individuals overseeing a company's direction, strategy, and accountability. Commonly employed by shareholders, executives, and those who love formal voting sessions in fancy rooms.

"Our board of directors demanded growth—no one mentioned profit, just growth. Growth at all costs."

Related Terms: Executive summary, Rubber stamp

BOIL THE OCEAN

phrase. Attempting to accomplish something overwhelmingly broad or complex, beyond practical limits. Commonly employed by project leads, strategists, and executives warning against overly ambitious scope.

"Our marketing plan tried to boil the ocean—turns out global domination isn't a Q2 deliverable."

Related Terms: Don't boil the ocean, Scope creep, Bubble mentality

BOILING THE OCEAN

phrase. Another form of "boil the ocean," emphasizing the attempt to tackle an impossibly large task. Commonly employed similarly by critics and observers noting absurdly grand ambitions.

"By boiling the ocean, we spent more time evaporating resources than producing results."

Related Terms: Boil the ocean, Over-engineering, Mission critical

BOOTSTRAPPING

n. Launching and growing a business with minimal external funding, relying on internal resources. Commonly employed by entrepreneurs, founders, and optimists who prefer personal savings to VCs.

"We're bootstrapping the startup, meaning the coffee budget equals last week's leftover grounds."

Related Terms: Angel investor, Unicorn, Lean startup

BOTTLENECK

n. A point of congestion or delay that slows down the entire process. Commonly employed by project managers, ops teams, and anyone diagnosing workflow issues.

"Our production line had a bottleneck so severe that even molasses in winter could outrun our workflow."

Related Terms: Broken workflow, Process fatigue

BOTTOM FEEDER

n. A person or company thriving by exploiting others' mistakes or misfortunes. Commonly employed by critics describing opportunistic consultants or competitors.

"The consultant was a bottom feeder, swooping in to profit from our screw-ups like a seagull at a trash heap."

Related Terms: Chainsaw consultant, Cutthroat

BOUNDARY CONDITIONS

(Noun) The constraints or parameters that limit the scope of a project, decision, or analysis, defining what's inside the sandbox and what's off-limits. Commonly employed by strategists, project leads, and engineers who prefer neat boxes over chaotic free-for-alls.

"Before proposing that global takeover, let's check our boundary conditions—like the fact we have zero budget."

Related Terms: Boil the ocean, Nail jelly to the wall, Scope creep

BRAIN DUMP

n. Rapidly listing out all one's thoughts or ideas in no particular order. Commonly employed by teams at the start of projects to organize scattered information.

"I gave a brain dump of my ideas in the meeting, which felt more like a confetti cannon of half-baked concepts."

Related Terms: Deep dive, Ideate

BREAK DOWN SILOS

phrase. Removing barriers between departments to foster cross-team collaboration. Commonly employed by executives and leaders frustrated by poor communication between units.

"We tried to break down silos, but management preferred silos—it makes it easier to blame someone else later."

Related Terms: Silo, Silo mentality, Cross-channel marketing

BRING IT TO THE TABLE

phrase. Presenting skills, expertise, or value to a discussion or project. Commonly employed by hiring managers, team leads, and collaborators evaluating contributions.

"They asked what I bring to the table, so I showed up with coffee and sarcasm, which is more than most here provide."

Related Terms: Core competencies, Value proposition, Aces in their places

BRING TO THE TABLE

phrase. Similar to above, referencing the particular talents or capabilities one offers. Commonly employed by HR and leadership assessing a candidate's worth.

"HR asked what I bring to the table—apparently 'well-timed eye rolls' was not the skill set they had in mind."

Related Terms: Core competency, Skillset, Culture fit

BROKEN RECORD

n. Repeating the same message so often it becomes tiresome. Commonly employed by colleagues describing repetitive management communications.

"Our VP sounded like a broken record about 'innovation,' yet we're still selling the same stale product."

Related Terms: Mission critical, Groundhog Day

BROKEN WORKFLOW

n. An inefficient or disrupted sequence of processes that halts progress or productivity. Commonly employed by process analysts, ops teams, and anyone suffering delays.

"Our broken workflow ensures that instead of producing results, we produce excuses at record speed."

Related Terms: Bottleneck, Process fatigue

BROWNFIELD SITE

n. Previously developed industrial land that may be contaminated and requires remediation before use. Commonly employed in real estate development and urban planning.

"Turning that brownfield site into offices was ambitious, like planting daisies in a toxic swamp and hoping for a garden party."

Related Terms: Greenfield site, Real estate bubble

BUBBLE MENTALITY

n. Operating in isolation from external perspectives, fostering a false sense of security. Commonly employed by managers warning about groupthink or closed-off corporate cultures.

"We developed a bubble mentality so airtight we believed our mediocre app was the next iPhone."

Related Terms: Silo mentality, Mushroom management

BUCKETS

n. Categories or classifications used to organize data, tasks, or resources. Commonly employed by analysts, PMs, and organizers to structure work.

"We divided the project into buckets, then promptly drowned in them because we forgot to assign anyone a life jacket."

Related Terms: Matrices, Framework, Granular

BUILD-TO-SUIT

phrase. Constructing a building tailored to a specific tenant's requirements. Commonly employed in commercial real estate and property management.

"We offered build-to-suit, meaning we'll pretend to care about your 'unique vision' before we make it look like every other boxy office."

Related Terms: Tenant improvement, Real estate development

BUILDING CODE

n. Regulations governing building design, construction, and maintenance. Commonly employed by architects, contractors, and property developers ensuring compliance.

"We tried to skirt building code like it was a polite suggestion, until the inspector showed up with a magnifying glass and a grin."

Related Terms: Zoning laws, Green building

BULLSHIT BINGO

n. A game played during meetings where participants mark off overused jargon or buzzwords. Commonly employed by bored employees silently mocking corporate speak.

"Our meeting was so full of synergy and low-hanging fruit that I won bullshit bingo in record time."

Related Terms: Corporate lingo, Management speak

BUNDLED PAYMENTS

n. A healthcare payment model where one set price covers multiple related services. Commonly employed by healthcare payers, providers, and policy analysts aiming at cost efficiency.

"Bundled payments sounded efficient until the hospital bundled my flu shot with a random kidney scan."

Related Terms: Accountable care organization (ACO), Value-based care

BUREAUCRATIC INEFFICIENCY

n. The ineffectiveness caused by complex regulations, forms, and slow processes. Commonly employed by critics of large organizations or government bodies.

"Our request got lost in bureaucratic inefficiency, proving that a thousand forms can stall even the simplest idea."

Related Terms: Bureaucratic inertia, Bureaucratic red tape, Regulatory compliance

BUREAUCRATIC INERTIA

n. The tendency of bureaucracy to resist change, maintaining the status quo. Commonly employed by employees frustrated with rigid structures and slow decision-making.

"Proposing a new process here is like asking a glacier to sprint—bureaucratic inertia doesn't do 'forward.'"

Related Terms: Bureaucratic inefficiency, Bureaucratic red tape

BUREAUCRATIC RED TAPE

n. Excessive regulations and formalities delaying decisions and actions. Commonly employed by anyone exasperated with unnecessary paperwork.

"We tried to buy new pens, but bureaucratic red tape required a 10-page justification and a blood oath."

Related Terms: Bureaucratic inefficiency, Bureaucratic inertia, Regulatory capture

BURN RATE

n. The rate at which a company spends its capital, often cited in startups. Commonly employed by CFOs, founders, and investors evaluating financial health.

"Our burn rate was so high we might as well light our cash on fire to keep warm in the boardroom."

Related Terms: Dry powder

BURNING BRIDGES

phrase. Destroying relationships or connections beyond repair. Commonly employed by managers and mentors warning against leaving on bad terms.

"She burned so many bridges on her last day that the fire department subscribed to her LinkedIn."

Related Terms: Exit strategy, Hostage mentality

BURNOUT

n. Extreme exhaustion caused by prolonged stress and overwork, reducing productivity and morale. Commonly employed by HR, team leads, and wellness advocates.

"I reached burnout when I started daydreaming about fax machines as an escape from email hell."

Related Terms: Busy work, Death march, Workstream

BUSINESS CASE

n. The rationale or justification for starting a project or venture, often including cost-benefit analysis. Commonly employed by executives and project managers to secure approval or funding.

"Our business case for the new product was basically 'If we build it, maybe someone will buy it, please?'"

Related Terms: ROI (Return on Investment), Cost-benefit analysis, Go-to-market strategy

BUSINESS TRANSFORMATION

n. Fundamental changes to a company's operations, culture, or processes to improve performance. Commonly employed by leadership teams aiming for strategic shifts and competitiveness.

"Our business transformation plan involved rearranging deck chairs while the Titanic sank—truly visionary."

Related Terms: 2.0, Change management, Digital transformation

BUSINESS-AS-USUAL (BAU) TRAP

n. Continuing routine operations even when change is needed, causing stagnation. Commonly employed by critics warning against complacency and lack of innovation.

"We're stuck in the BAU trap, refusing to acknowledge that 'the way we've always done it' is code for 'we're doomed.'"

Related Terms: Resistance to change, Status quo bias

BUSY WORK

n. Tasks that keep people occupied without producing meaningful results. Commonly employed by managers (unintentionally) or arises in bureaucratic environments.

"They gave me busy work so pointless I wondered if I was part of a secret social experiment on time-wasting."

Related Terms: Burnout, Flogging a dead horse

BUY-IN

n. Agreement or support from stakeholders or team members for a plan or decision. Commonly employed by leaders trying to ensure everyone is committed to a strategy.

"Getting buy-in for the new initiative was easier than expected—everyone signed off so they could leave early."

Related Terms: Stakeholder engagement, Consensus building

BUYER'S AGENT

n. A real estate agent representing the buyer in a property transaction. Commonly employed by homebuyers seeking expert guidance and negotiation support.

"Our buyer's agent tried to act interested as we pointed out every flaw, probably while counting their commission."

Related Terms: Listing agent, Investment property

C

IS FOR CORE COMPETENCIES BECAUSE COUNTING ON CORE COMPETENCIES CREATES COMPETITIVE CLOUT—C'MON, CULTIVATE WHAT YOU'RE GOOD AT!

COB (CLOSE OF BUSINESS)

abbr. Typically means by 5:00 PM, indicating a deadline by the end of the workday. Commonly employed by managers, colleagues, and clients to set short-term deadlines.

"When they say 'submit by COB,' they really mean 'Procrastinate until 4:59 and panic.'"

Related Terms: EOD (End Of Day), ASAP (As Soon As Possible)

CPA (COST PER ACQUISITION)

abbr. The cost to acquire a new customer, often calculated in marketing or sales efforts. Commonly employed by marketers, advertisers, and CFOs evaluating campaign efficiency.

"Our CPA was so high we'd have saved money handing out $50 bills on the street corner."

Related Terms: Conversion rate, ROI (Return on Investment)

CYA (COVER YOUR ASS)

abbr. Actions taken to avoid blame or negative consequences, often involving excessive documentation. Commonly employed by employees and managers in risk-averse or political environments.

"Our reports were full of disclaimers, a classic CYA move to dodge the fallout when things collapse."

Related Terms: Due diligence, Risk management

CADENCE

n. The regular schedule or rhythm at which meetings, updates, or processes occur. Commonly employed by project managers and team leads to ensure steady progress.

"We have a weekly cadence of meetings so repetitive they could replace white noise machines."

Related Terms: Timebox, Break down silos, Consensus building

CAN OF WORMS

n. A small issue that, when addressed, leads to a much larger and more complex problem. Commonly employed by teams warning against opening topics that trigger complications.

"Asking about pay raises opened a can of worms so huge we needed pest control."

Related Terms: Scope creep, Flogging a dead horse

CANARY IN THE COAL MINE

n. An early warning sign of potential trouble, referencing old mining practice. Commonly employed by managers, analysts, and strategists noting early red flags.

"When our only loyal customer left a one-star review, it was the canary in the coal mine for our brand."

Related Terms: Bubble mentality, Counterfactual

CANARY IN THE COALMINE

n. Variation of the above phrase, another early warning sign metaphor. Commonly employed similarly to "canary in the coal mine."

"The sudden drop in web traffic was our canary in the coalmine, telling us our content strategy was as appealing as stale bread."

Related Terms: Canary in the coal mine, Churn, Conversion rate

CAP RATE (CAPITALIZATION RATE)

n. A measure of return on a real estate investment based on its net income and value. Commonly employed by real estate investors and analysts evaluating property deals.

"The cap rate looked great on paper until we realized 'net income' was a mythical creature in this neighborhood."

Related Terms: Investment property, 1031 exchange, Real estate development

CAPACITY BUILDING

n. Efforts to improve an organization's effectiveness, resources, and sustainability. Commonly employed by nonprofits, NGOs, and developmental agencies.

"Our capacity building efforts taught us how to do more with less, which is code for 'Cut corners gracefully.'"

Related Terms: Nonprofit sector, Change management, Business transformation

CAPACITY CONSTRAINTS

n. Limitations preventing an organization from meeting demand efficiently. Commonly employed by operations, supply chain managers, and planners.

"Our capacity constraints were so tight we couldn't supply a lemonade stand without a six-month waitlist."

Related Terms: Bottleneck, Broken workflow, Lean methodology

CAPITAL CAMPAIGN

n. A targeted fundraising effort aimed at raising large sums for a specific project. Commonly employed by nonprofits, educational institutions, and foundations.

"Our capital campaign's big idea: guilt everyone into donating until we can afford that shiny new lobby."

Related Terms: Charitable giving, 501(c)(3), Donor stewardship

CAPITALIZATION RATE (CAP RATE)

n. Same as cap rate, a key metric for evaluating real estate investments. Commonly employed by investors and analysts in property valuation.

"We bragged about a high cap rate, conveniently ignoring that no one actually wants to buy our overhyped property."

Related Terms: Cap rate (Capitalization rate), 1031 exchange, REIT (Real Estate Investment Trust)

CAPITATION

n. A healthcare payment model where providers receive a fixed amount per patient regardless of services used. Commonly employed by insurers and healthcare providers managing costs and care.

"Under capitation, doctors get paid whether they see you or not—truly the Netflix subscription of healthcare."

Related Terms: Accountable care organization (ACO), Bundled payments, Value-based care

CARBON PRICING

n. Charging businesses or entities for carbon emissions to incentivize reduction. Commonly employed by policymakers, governments, and sustainability officers.

"Our CFO sobbed quietly when they introduced carbon pricing, as if balancing the environment and profits was a personal insult."

Related Terms: Corporate social responsibility (CSR), Sustainability, Environmental impact assessment (EIA)

CARE COORDINATION

n. Organizing patient care activities and sharing information among healthcare participants for better outcomes. Commonly employed by healthcare systems, ACOs, and case managers.

"Care coordination aimed to streamline treatment, but it felt more like passing the patient around like a hot potato."

Related Terms: Chronic care management, Accountable care organization (ACO), Value-based care

CASE STUDY

n. An in-depth analysis of a particular project, customer, or situation to understand results. Commonly employed by marketers, consultants, and researchers to illustrate success or failure.

"Our case study proved that, yes, failing spectacularly is indeed a viable outcome if you ignore all warnings."

Related Terms: Deep dive, Counterfactual

CENSUS DATA

n. Government-collected population statistics used for analysis and decision-making. Commonly employed by researchers, planners, and policy analysts.

"We analyzed census data to learn that our customers are people with pulses—insightful!"

Related Terms: Citizen feedback, Public policy, Market analysis

CHAINSAW CONSULTANT

n. A business advisor known for aggressive cost-cutting measures, often ruthlessly applied. Commonly employed (reluctantly) by companies seeking rapid expense reduction.

"The chainsaw consultant recommended layoffs and selling the coffee machine—apparently morale is overrated."

Related Terms: Bottom feeder, Cutthroat, Burn rate

CHAIR

n. The person responsible for organizing and leading a meeting or committee. Commonly employed by boards, committees, and teams needing clear leadership in discussions.

"As chair, I guided the meeting into a swamp of indecision, then adjourned before anyone noticed my incompetence."

Related Terms: Consensus building, Facipulate, Committee / Taskforce / Working Group

CHAMPION

n. A supporter or advocate who promotes and defends a project, product, or idea. Commonly employed by project leads, managers, or sponsors who need internal allies.

"Our project champion cheered us on right up until the budget got slashed, then quietly vanished."

Related Terms: Buy-in, Stakeholder engagement, Change management

CHANGE MANAGEMENT

n. Approaches and strategies to guide organizations through transitions, ensuring buy-in and minimizing disruption. Commonly employed by HR, consultants, and leadership during restructuring or transformations.

"Our change management plan involved inspirational quotes and mandatory positivity training—shockingly ineffective."

Related Terms: Business transformation, Consensus building, Resistance to change

CHARITABLE GIVING

n. Donations of money or resources to charitable organizations. Commonly employed by nonprofits, donors, and CSR initiatives.

"We bragged about charitable giving, ignoring that our donation was just last year's expired promotional t-shirts."

Related Terms: 501(c)(3), Capital campaign, Nonprofit sector

CHATHAM HOUSE RULES

n. A meeting principle allowing participants to use information but not identify the speakers. Commonly employed by organizations aiming for open discussion without attributing comments.

"Under Chatham House Rules, we can gossip freely about our clueless VP, as long as we pretend we don't know who said what."

Related Terms: Consensus building, Facipulate, Transparency

CHIME IN

v. To join a conversation or discussion by offering thoughts or ideas. Commonly employed by team members in brainstorming sessions or meetings.

"I chimed in with a suggestion only to realize everyone wanted me to remain a decorative potted plant."

Related Terms: Brain dump, Ideate, Circle back

CHRONIC CARE MANAGEMENT

n. Coordinated healthcare services for patients with ongoing chronic conditions. Commonly employed by care coordinators, case managers, and integrated delivery systems.

"Chronic care management let us juggle doctors like clowns at a circus, hoping one might actually fix something."

Related Terms: Care coordination, Accountable care organization (ACO), Value-based care

CHURN

n. The rate at which employees, customers, or users leave an organization or stop using a service. Commonly employed by HR, marketing, and customer success teams tracking retention.

"Our churn rate was so high we considered installing a revolving door just for exiting staff."

Related Terms: Churn rate, User acquisition

CHURN RATE

n. The percentage of customers, users, or employees lost over a given period. Commonly employed by subscription businesses, HR analytics teams, and customer success professionals.

"We measured churn rate to confirm our suspicion: customers flee us faster than we can say 'loyalty program.'"

Related Terms: Churn, Conversion rate, FOMO (Fear Of Missing Out)

CIRCLE BACK

v. To revisit a topic or issue after gathering more information or waiting some time. Commonly employed by managers, project leads, and colleagues deferring discussions.

"We'll circle back on that suggestion, which is corporate speak for 'We'll ignore it until you forget.'"

Related Terms: Chime in, Deep dive, Stakeholder engagement

CITIZEN FEEDBACK

n. Opinions, suggestions, and input from the general public or community members. Commonly employed by government agencies, nonprofits, and civic groups.

"The committee asked for citizen feedback, then promptly filed it under 'Things to Never Read.'"

Related Terms: Census data, Public policy, Community outreach

CIVIL LIBERTIES

n. Fundamental rights and freedoms protected by law. Commonly employed in policy discussions, legal frameworks, and activist communities.

"Our meeting felt like a violation of civil liberties, forcing us to listen to hour-long PowerPoint monologues."

Related Terms: Chatham House Rules, Election integrity

CIVIL SERVICE

n. The permanent professional branches of government administration. Commonly employed by government agencies, public sector organizations, and HR departments in public jobs.

"Joining the civil service means trading your soul for a stable paycheck and a bureaucratic maze you call 'home.'"

Related Terms: Bureaucratic inertia, Bureaucratic red tape

CLICK-THROUGH RATE (CTR)

n. The percentage of users who click on a specific link or ad after seeing it. Commonly employed by digital marketers, advertisers, and campaign managers.

"Our CTR improved slightly when we replaced 'Buy Now!' with 'Please, we're desperate!'"

Related Terms: Conversion rate, A/B testing, Contextual targeting

CLIENT-CENTRIC

adj. Prioritizing the needs, preferences, and satisfaction of customers. Commonly employed by customer service teams, consultants, and marketers.

"We're totally client-centric—so long as the client's needs magically align with what's cheapest for us."

Related Terms: Customer-centric, User experience (UX)

CLIMBING A GREASY POLE

phrase. Striving for a difficult or highly competitive goal, often with sabotage or obstacles. Commonly employed by employees describing tough career advancement.

"Getting a promotion here is like climbing a greasy pole: you end up covered in slime and still at the bottom."

Related Terms: Cutthroat, Culture fit, HiPPO (Highest-Paid Person's Opinion)

CLINICAL DOCUMENTATION IMPROVEMENT (CDI)

n. Efforts to enhance the accuracy and completeness of patient medical records. Commonly employed by healthcare administrators, HIM professionals, and coding specialists.

"After CDI training, we learned that 'Patient seems off' is not considered a best-practice medical note."

Related Terms: Care coordination, Chronic care management, Value-based care

CLINICAL PATHWAYS

n. Standardized care plans outlining steps for treating specific conditions. Commonly employed by healthcare providers, hospitals, and quality improvement teams.

"Our clinical pathways guided care so rigidly that deviating by two steps risked a bureaucratic heart attack."

Related Terms: Care coordination, Accountable care organization (ACO), Capitation

CLINICAL TRIAL

n. Research studies testing new treatments or medications for safety and effectiveness. Commonly employed by pharmaceutical companies, researchers, and regulatory bodies.

"We entered a clinical trial that promised miracles, but mostly delivered questionnaires longer than Dostoevsky novels."

Related Terms: Deep dive, Case study, Regulatory compliance

CLOCK WATCHER

n. An employee who frequently checks the time, often indicating disengagement or boredom. Commonly employed by managers noting a lack of engagement in staff.

"Our intern became a clock watcher after realizing that '5 PM' was the real deliverable of the day."

Related Terms: Burnout, Busy work, Culture fit

CLOUD COMPUTING

n. Delivering computing services (servers, storage, databases) over the internet. Commonly employed by IT teams, SaaS providers, and companies needing scalable infrastructure.

"We moved to cloud computing, hoping to scale up easily, but ended up with bills so high we needed oxygen masks."

Related Terms: Cloud-based, SaaS (Software as a Service), Scalability

CLOUD-BASED

adj. Hosted and accessed via the internet rather than local hardware. Commonly employed by tech companies, IT admins, and software vendors.

"Our cloud-based solution crashed whenever it rained, adding irony to inconvenience."

Related Terms: Cloud computing, SaaS (Software as a Service), Scalability issues

COMMITTEE / TASKFORCE / WORKING GROUP

n. A group assembled to discuss and make decisions on specific topics or problems. Commonly employed by organizations needing collective input or governance structures.

"We formed a taskforce to study productivity, spending most of the time proving we have none."

Related Terms: Consensus building, Chair, Chatham House Rules

COMMONWEALTH

n. A political community organized for the common good, often a reference to certain governmental forms. Commonly employed in governmental contexts or historical references.

"In our office commonwealth, everyone shares the workload just enough to blame each other when it fails."

Related Terms: Civil service, Public sector, Government accountability

COMMUNITY OUTREACH

n. Efforts by nonprofits, governments, or companies to engage and serve local communities. Commonly employed by nonprofits, CSR programs, and local government agencies.

"Our community outreach involved handing out stale cookies while lecturing people on how grateful they should be."

Related Terms: Citizen feedback, Charitable giving, Nonprofit sector

CONSENSUS BUILDING

n. Achieving agreement among stakeholders or team members on a decision. Commonly employed by facilitators, team leads, and negotiators.

"Consensus building here means we nod politely, then do what the CEO already decided."

Related Terms: Chair, Stakeholder engagement, Change management

CONSULT

v. To seek someone's opinion, guidance, or expertise before making decisions. Commonly employed by managers, decision-makers, and professionals needing specialized input.

"We consulted the 'expert,' who gave us advice so generic we could print it on fortune cookies."

Related Terms: Due diligence, Fact pattern, Cost-benefit analysis

CONTEXT

n. The details, background, or circumstances necessary for fully understanding a situation. Commonly employed by managers, analysts, and team members before making informed decisions.

"Our manager demanded results without context, like asking a chef to cook a meal blindfolded in an empty pantry."

Related Terms: Deep dive, Case study, Brain dump

CONTEXTUAL TARGETING

n. Delivering ads based on the content of a webpage or app, rather than user behavior. Commonly employed by digital marketers and advertisers optimizing relevance.

"We tried contextual targeting so that when users read about saving money, we hit them with luxury car ads. Genius."

Related Terms: A/B testing, Conversion rate, Cookie tracking

CONVERSION RATE

n. The percentage of visitors or recipients who complete a desired action, like making a purchase. Commonly employed by marketers, product managers, and sales teams to measure success.

"Our conversion rate improved after we told customers: 'Buy now or we'll email you every hour forever.'"

Related Terms: A/B testing, Click-through rate (CTR), Churn rate

COOKIE TRACKING

n. Using cookies to track users' online activity for targeting or analytics purposes. Commonly employed by advertisers, marketers, and analytics teams.

"Thanks to cookie tracking, we know you looked at dog beds at 3 AM—now watch these dog food ads while you weep."

Related Terms: Contextual targeting, Conversion rate, Programmatic advertising

COOKIE-CUTTER APPROACH

n. A generic, one-size-fits-all method lacking customization or originality. Commonly employed by critics highlighting uninspired solutions.

"Our cookie-cutter approach to product design ensured every offering was equally bland and uninspiring."

Related Terms: Core competencies (contrast unique strengths), Low-hanging fruit, Lean methodology (aiming to remove waste, not be generic)

CORE COMPETENCIES

n. The skills or activities at which an individual or organization excels. Commonly employed by HR, consultants, and strategists focusing on competitive advantage.

"Our core competencies: wasting time, dodging accountability, and printing motivational posters no one reads."

Related Terms: Aces in their places, Bring it to the table, Core values

CORE VALUES

n. The guiding principles or standards influencing decisions and actions within an organization. Commonly employed by executives, HR, and branding teams shaping company culture.

"Our company's core values include 'integrity,' which we interpret as 'Don't get caught lying.'"

Related Terms: Culture fit, Mission statement, Corporate social responsibility (CSR)

COST-PER-CLICK (CPC)

n. An advertising model where payment occurs each time a user clicks on an ad. Commonly employed by advertisers, marketers, and online media buyers.

"Our CPC model meant every curious click drained our budget faster than a toddler grabbing candy."

Related Terms: Cost-per-impression (CPM), A/B testing, Conversion rate

COST-PER-IMPRESSION (CPM)

n. An advertising model charging per thousand ad impressions shown. Commonly employed by digital advertisers and publishers.

"CPM let us pay for the privilege of being ignored by even more people at scale."

Related Terms: Cost-per-click (CPC), Programmatic advertising, Viewability

COUNTERFACTUAL

n. An imagined scenario different from the current reality, used for analysis or hypothesis testing. Commonly employed by strategists, analysts, and researchers probing "what-if" situations.

"In a counterfactual world, our product launch wasn't a dumpster fire, but here we are with a charred marketing plan."

Related Terms: Case study, Deep dive, Canary in the coal mine

CREATIVE MANAGEMENT PLATFORM (CMP)

n. Software for designing, managing, and optimizing ad creatives. Commonly employed by marketing teams seeking streamlined ad production and testing.

"We got a CMP to prove we love data, or at least to pretend we know what to do with it."

Related Terms: A/B testing, Programmatic advertising, Data management platform (DMP)

CRISIS MANAGEMENT

n. Preparing for and responding effectively to emergencies or disasters. Commonly employed by PR, executive teams, and risk management professionals.

"Our crisis management strategy is yelling 'Stay calm!' while everything burns and we hide under the conference table."

Related Terms: Crisis mode, Risk management, Change management

CRISIS MODE

n. A state of constantly reacting to problems without a stable plan. Commonly employed by teams overwhelmed by fires to fight, lacking strategic calm.

"We lived in crisis mode so long, we forgot what normal looked like—if it ever existed."

Related Terms: Crisis management, Death march, Drinking from the firehose

CRITICAL CARE

n. Specialized, intensive medical treatment for life-threatening conditions. Commonly employed in healthcare, ICUs, and emergency medicine.

"We gave our failing project critical care, which meant quietly staring at it and hoping it would heal itself."

Related Terms: Chronic care management, Care coordination, Value-based care

CRITICAL PATH

n. The sequence of key tasks determining the shortest possible completion time in a project. Commonly employed by project managers scheduling work efficiently.

"We identified the critical path just so we could block it with endless revisions and bureaucracy."

Related Terms: Bottleneck, Timebox, Deliverable

CROSS-CHANNEL MARKETING

n. Using multiple marketing channels to reach customers consistently and coherently. Commonly employed by marketers seeking broader reach and integrated campaigns.

"Our cross-channel marketing ensured customers were annoyed by us equally on email, social media, and direct mail."

Related Terms: Contextual targeting, A/B testing, Branding (If "Branding" not defined, skip. Let's pick Conversion rate)

Revised Related Terms: Contextual targeting, A/B testing, Conversion rate

CROSS-DEVICE TRACKING

n. Tracking users across multiple devices for better targeting and analytics. Commonly employed by advertisers, data analysts, and tech companies.

"With cross-device tracking, we stalk your browsing habits from your phone to your fridge's touchscreen—privacy, what's that?"

Related Terms: Cookie tracking, Programmatic advertising, DMP (Data management platform)

CROWD-FUNDED INVESTMENT

n. Funding a project by raising small contributions from many individuals online. Commonly employed by startups, nonprofits, and small businesses seeking alternative financing.

"We tried crowd-funded investment, hoping strangers online would throw money at us like a poorly managed GoFundMe."

Related Terms: Crowdfunding, Capital campaign, Nonprofit sector

CROWDFUNDING

n. Raising capital from a large number of people, typically via online platforms. Commonly employed by startups, creators, and nonprofits seeking grassroots support.

"Our crowdfunding campaign aimed to raise $50,000 but got $50 and a note saying 'good luck, losers.'"

Related Terms: Crowd-funded investment, Capital campaign, FOMO (Fear Of Missing Out)

CRYPTO WALLET

n. A digital wallet for storing, sending, and receiving cryptocurrencies. Commonly employed by crypto traders, investors, and blockchain enthusiasts.

"My crypto wallet held coins so valuable that one market dip turned my Lambo dreams into a moped reality."

Related Terms: DeFi (Decentralized Finance), DApps (Decentralized applications)

CULTURE FIT

n. Hiring people who align with the existing team's values and work style (often limiting diversity). Commonly employed by HR, recruiters, and hiring managers.

"We prioritize 'culture fit,' which is HR code for 'clones only, no original thoughts allowed.'"

Related Terms: Core values, Aces in their places, Bring to the table

CUSTOMER JOURNEY

n. The process customers go through from initial awareness to purchase and beyond. Commonly employed by marketers, UX designers, and product teams.

"Our customer journey felt like a labyrinth of pop-ups and broken links—an epic quest for anyone who dares to unsubscribe."

Related Terms: Customer journey mapping, Conversion rate, Client-centric

CUSTOMER JOURNEY MAPPING

n. Visualizing the steps customers take, helping identify improvements in marketing or service delivery. Commonly employed by UX, marketing, and customer success teams.

"After customer journey mapping, we found that 90% bail at Step 2, presumably to preserve their sanity."

Related Terms: Customer journey, A/B testing, User experience (UX)

CUSTOMER-CENTRIC

adj. Focusing on customers' needs, experiences, and satisfaction above all else. Commonly employed by companies striving to differentiate via excellent service.

"We're totally customer-centric: we'll even pretend to listen to their complaints before ignoring them."

Related Terms: Client-centric, Customer journey, User experience (UX)

CUTTHROAT

adj. Describing a highly competitive environment where individuals may harm others to get ahead. Commonly employed by employees describing hostile sales floors or competitive workplaces.

"Our sales floor is so cutthroat that shaking hands might require a tetanus shot afterward."

Related Terms: Bottom feeder, Chainsaw consultant, Climbing a greasy pole

CUTTING CORNERS

phrase. Taking shortcuts that reduce quality or thoroughness. Commonly employed by critics noting a drop in standards to save time or money.

"We cut so many corners the project turned into a perfect circle of disappointment."

Related Terms: Busy work, Lean methodology, Burnout

D

IS FOR DISRUPTION BECAUSE DOUBLING DOWN ON DISRUPTION DELIGHTS DARING DREAMERS—DON'T DILUTE YOUR DYNAMITE!

DNB (DO NOT BOTHER/BOOK)

abbr. Used to mark unavailability or block off time on calendars. Commonly employed by employees and managers needing focus time or privacy.

"I marked 'DNB' on my calendar, but my boss read it as 'Double New Burdens, please!'"

Related Terms: Timebox, F2F (Face-to-Face), Cadence

DATA MANAGEMENT PLATFORM (DMP)

n. Software collecting, organizing, and analyzing data for better ad targeting and insights. Commonly employed by marketers, data scientists, and digital advertisers.

"We got a DMP to prove we love data, or at least to pretend we know what to do with it."

Related Terms: Creative management platform (CMP), Cookie tracking, Programmatic advertising

DEFI (DECENTRALIZED FINANCE)

abbr. Financial services without traditional intermediaries, powered by blockchain technology. Commonly employed by crypto enthusiasts, fintech innovators, and early adopters.

"In DeFi, we replaced banks with code and hype, ensuring we can lose money at the speed of technology."

Related Terms: Crypto wallet, DApps (Decentralized applications)

DEAD WEIGHT

n. An unproductive individual adding little value to a team or project. Commonly employed by managers and team members identifying slackers.

"Bob was dead weight, contributing less than the office fern, which at least purified the air."

Related Terms: Donkey work, Busy work, Cutting corners

DEATH BY POWERPOINT

phrase. Overwhelming audiences with too many slides or too much information in a presentation. Commonly employed by bored attendees mocking lengthy decks.

"Our training was death by PowerPoint; by slide 100, I was praying for a tech glitch to free me."

Related Terms: Deck, Broken record, Dumpster fire

DEATH BY A THOUSAND CUTS

phrase. Many small problems accumulating to cause failure. Commonly employed by managers and teams noting slow, incremental damage.

"Our product launch faced death by a thousand cuts: minor bugs, missing packaging, and a CEO who overslept."

Related Terms: Scope creep, Bottleneck, Misalignment of objectives

DEATH MARCH

n. A project doomed to fail due to unrealistic expectations or poor planning. Commonly employed by developers, project managers, and employees stuck in hopeless efforts.

"We trudged through the death march project, bonding over shared misery like survivors in a bad horror flick."

Related Terms: Burnout, Crisis mode, Death by a thousand cuts

DEATH SPIRAL

n. A situation worsening continuously until collapse. Commonly employed by analysts describing failing businesses or spiraling problems.

"After the second recall, the company entered a death spiral so obvious even the interns bet against us."

Related Terms: Death march, Dumpster fire, Churn

DEBT CEILING

n. A government-imposed limit on how much debt the country can incur.

Commonly employed by policymakers, economists, and media discussing fiscal policy.

"Arguing about the debt ceiling is like debating if the credit card maxes out at 'Doomed' or 'Totally Screwed.'"

Related Terms: Fiscal policy, Economic stimulus, Government procurement

DECENTRALIZED APPLICATIONS (DAPPS)

n. Apps running on a decentralized network (e.g., blockchain) without a central authority. Commonly employed by blockchain developers, crypto users, and Web3 enthusiasts.

"Our DApp promised freedom and transparency, but mostly delivered confusion and a new set of buzzwords."

Related Terms: DeFi (Decentralized Finance), Crypto wallet, Tokenomics

DECK

n. A presentation, typically in PowerPoint or similar format. Commonly employed by presenters, salespeople, and consultants.

"Our investor deck contained more fluff than a cotton candy machine that exploded."

Related Terms: Death by PowerPoint, Pitch deck, Management speak

DEEP DIVE

n. A comprehensive, detailed examination of a subject. Commonly employed by analysts, researchers, and project teams seeking thorough understanding.

"We did a deep dive into customer feedback, discovering they hate us in increasingly creative ways."

Related Terms: Case study, Counterfactual, Brain dump

DEEP LEARNING

n. A subset of machine learning using complex neural networks that improve with large amounts of data. Commonly employed by data scientists, AI researchers, and tech companies developing predictive models.

"Our deep learning model claimed it could predict trends, but mostly it predicted we'd regret this investment."

Related Terms: Machine Learning, Data management platform (DMP), Innovation

DELIVERABLE

n. A tangible outcome or piece of work that must be completed as part of a project. Commonly employed by project managers and stakeholders defining project outputs.

"My only deliverable was a two-page report, which I turned into a 50-slide deck for maximum eye-rolling."

Related Terms: Deliverables, Scope, Critical path

DELTA

n. The difference or change between two values or conditions. Commonly employed by analysts, finance professionals, and scientists comparing outcomes.

"We measured the delta in profits, which was like measuring the height of a sinkhole where our money used to be."

Related Terms: Cost-benefit analysis, KPI (Key Performance Indicator), Conversion rate

DEMAND-SIDE PLATFORM (DSP)

n. A platform enabling advertisers to buy ad inventory across multiple publishers in real-time. Commonly employed by advertisers, media buyers, and digital marketing teams.

"We used a DSP to get 'premium' ad spots, which somehow ended up next to clickbait for miracle diets."

Related Terms: Programmatic advertising, Data management platform (DMP), Creative management platform (CMP)

DEPRECIATION

n. The decrease in a property's or asset's value over time. Commonly employed by accountants, finance teams, and tax professionals.

"My car's value experienced depreciation so dramatic it felt personal."

Related Terms: Cap rate (Capitalization rate), 1031 exchange, Cost-benefit analysis

DIAGNOSTIC-RELATED GROUPS (DRGS)

n. A system for classifying hospital cases to determine payments and costs. Commonly employed by insurers, hospitals, and healthcare administrators.

"DRGs helped insurers classify my hospital stay as 'too expensive, stop whining and pay up.'"

Related Terms: Capitation, Bundled payments, Value-based care

DIGITAL DIVIDE

n. The gap between those with and without access to modern technology or the internet. Commonly employed by policymakers, educators, and nonprofits addressing inequality.

"Our marketing team ignored the digital divide, sending fancy online surveys to people who think Wi-Fi is a snack."

Related Terms: Community outreach, Public policy, E-Government 2.0

DIGITAL TRANSFORMATION

n. Integrating digital technology into all areas of a business, fundamentally changing operations. Commonly employed by executives, CIOs, and consultants modernizing organizations.

"Our digital transformation strategy: install a chatbot and call it a day."

Related Terms: Business transformation, Change management, 2.0

DISRUPTION

n. Innovations that significantly alter traditional business models or markets. Commonly employed by startups, investors, and tech leaders praising game-changing ideas.

"We claimed 'disruption' every time we launched a half-baked feature, hoping investors wouldn't notice it was just chaos."

Related Terms: Disruptive, Innovation, Go to market

DISRUPTIVE

adj. Describing innovations that create new markets or displace established solutions. Commonly employed by marketers, CEOs, and VCs boasting about breakthrough products.

"Our CEO promised a disruptive product, but all we got was a glitchy app that disrupted our sanity."

Related Terms: Disruption, Innovation, Venture capital (VC)

DIVE RIGHT IN

phrase. To begin a task immediately and enthusiastically. Commonly employed by managers encouraging quick starts or proactive team members.

"They told me to dive right in, so I belly-flopped into a project with zero instructions and even less encouragement."

Related Terms: Circle back, Brain dump, Chime in

DOG-EAT-DOG

adj. A ruthlessly competitive environment where individuals may harm others to succeed. Commonly employed by employees describing harsh sales floors or cutthroat industries.

"Our sales team is dog-eat-dog, so I wore a meat suit to blend in."

Related Terms: Cutthroat, Climbing a greasy pole, Chainsaw consultant

DONKEY WORK

n. Boring, repetitive, or menial tasks considered low-value. Commonly employed by employees complaining about mundane duties.

"I spent the afternoon on donkey work—filing papers no one will read and sorting emails no one will answer."

Related Terms: Busy work, Dead weight, Flogging a dead horse

DONOR ADVISED FUND (DAF)

n. A philanthropic vehicle allowing donors to contribute and recommend grants over time. Commonly employed by wealthy donors, foundations, and charitable advisors.

"Our donor advised fund felt like a fancy piggy bank for guilt-ridden millionaires."

Related Terms: Charitable giving, Capital campaign, Donor stewardship

DONOR DATABASE

n. A system for storing and managing donor information in nonprofits. Commonly employed by fundraising teams, donor relations specialists, and charity administrators.

"Our donor database was so outdated we celebrated when it didn't crash upon opening."

Related Terms: Donor advised fund (DAF), Nonprofit compliance, Donor stewardship

DONOR RECOGNITION

n. Acknowledging and thanking donors for their contributions. Commonly employed by nonprofits, fundraising teams, and development officers.

"Our donor recognition included a framed thank-you and a newsletter shout-out they'll never read."

Related Terms: Charitable giving, Donor advised fund (DAF), Donor stewardship

DONOR STEWARDSHIP

n. Managing donor relationships to ensure continued support and long-term engagement. Commonly employed by nonprofits, fundraisers, and donor relations teams.

"With donor stewardship, we nurtured a relationship strong enough that they didn't ask for receipts—perfect."

Related Terms: Donor recognition, Donor advised fund (DAF), 501(c)(3)

DON'T BOIL THE OCEAN

phrase. A reminder not to attempt overly broad or unrealistic tasks. Commonly employed by project leads and managers cautioning against excessive scope.

"The boss said 'don't boil the ocean,' but then assigned us a project that's basically global desalination."

Related Terms: Scope creep, Cost-benefit analysis, Flogging a dead horse

DOTTED LINE VS. SOLID LINE (REPORTING)

n. Dotted line indicates shared or indirect responsibility; solid line indicates direct authority. Commonly employed by HR, organizational designers, and managers clarifying reporting structures.

"I report to my boss with a dotted line, which is just a polite way of saying 'I have zero actual power.'"

Related Terms: Change management, Aces in their places (role clarity), Break down silos

DOUBLE CLICK

(Verb) To explore or examine a topic in more detail, as if zooming in on a digital interface by double-clicking. Commonly employed by consultants, project leads, and bosses who think tech metaphors make them sound savvy.

"Let's double click on that sales data—because apparently saying 'look closer' is too old-fashioned."

Related Terms: Deep dive, Drill down, Marinate

DOWNTIME

n. Periods when systems, machinery, or staff are not operational or productive. Commonly employed by IT, operations, and maintenance teams planning schedules.

"We cherished downtime like a rare bird sighting—until someone asked us to do more 'thought leadership.'"

Related Terms: DNB (Do Not Bother/Book), Burnout, Workflow

DRAGGING YOUR FEET

phrase. Deliberately delaying or avoiding action. Commonly employed by supervisors or colleagues noting reluctance or procrastination.

"We dragged our feet on the new policy so long that a snail could have lapped us twice."

Related Terms: ALAP (As Late As Possible), Resistance to change, Scope creep

DRILL DOWN

v. Examining something in greater detail or depth. Commonly employed by analysts, managers, and team leads focusing on specifics.

"When we drilled down into the data, we discovered all our 'insights' were just guesswork with fancy charts."

Related Terms: Deep dive, Brain dump, A/B testing

DRINK THE KOOL-AID

phrase. Believing in an idea or principle without critical examination. Commonly employed by employees describing unquestioning adoption of company culture or strategy.

"Everyone drank the Kool-Aid about our 'game-changing' platform, which changed no games and ended none of my suffering."

Related Terms: Bubble mentality, Culture fit, HiPPO (Highest-Paid Person's Opinion)

DRINKING FROM THE FIREHOSE

phrase. Being overwhelmed by too much information or work at once. Commonly employed by new hires, interns, and teams handling rapid growth.

"Interns here learn by drinking from the firehose, which basically means drowning in chaos day one."

Related Terms: Crisis mode, Deep dive, Burnout

DROP THE BALL

phrase. To make an error or fail to complete a task successfully. Commonly employed by managers and colleagues noting accountability failures.

"We dropped the ball so hard it left a crater in Q4's revenue projections."

Related Terms: CYA (Cover Your Ass), Critical path, Deliverable

DRY POWDER

n. Additional funds or resources kept in reserve for future use. Commonly employed by investors, CFOs, and leadership preparing for opportunities or emergencies.

"Our CFO bragged about dry powder, but when trouble hit, we discovered he meant the stale cookies in the break room."

Related Terms: Burn rate, Crisis management

DUCKS IN A ROW

phrase. Being well organized and prepared. Commonly employed by project managers, team leads, and planners emphasizing readiness.

"We tried to get our ducks in a row, but the ducks had unionized and demanded a strategic plan first."

Related Terms: Scope, Critical path, Deliverables

DUE DILIGENCE

n. A thorough investigation or review conducted before making a major decision or investment. Commonly employed by investors, buyers, and compliance officers to minimize risk.

"Our due diligence on the new vendor consisted of a quick Google search and a shrug, so what could possibly go wrong?"

Related Terms: Cost-benefit analysis, CYA (Cover Your Ass), Regulatory compliance

DUMPSTER FIRE

n. A situation that has gone disastrously wrong. Commonly employed by employees, commentators, or the media describing total chaos.

"Our product launch was a dumpster fire, only with fewer marshmallows and more panicked screaming."

Related Terms: Death spiral, Crisis mode, Disruption

DYNAMIC CREATIVE OPTIMIZATION (DCO)

n. Automatically adjusting ad creative based on user data and context. Commonly employed by digital advertisers, programmatic buyers, and marketing teams.

"Thanks to DCO, we showed users ads so 'personalized' they wondered if we'd moved into their living room."

Related Terms: A/B testing, Creative management platform (CMP), Programmatic advertising

DYNAMIC PRICING

n. Adjusting prices based on demand, inventory, or other factors in real-time. Commonly employed by airlines, hotels, and online retailers seeking optimal revenue.

"We adopted dynamic pricing, so now our prices fluctuate faster than my mood on a Monday morning."

Related Terms: Conversion rate, Disruption, Scalability

E

IS FOR ECOSYSTEM BECAUSE ESTABLISHING AN EFFECTIVE ECOSYSTEM ENSURES ENDLESS EXPANSION—EMBRACE EVERYONE ENGAGING IN YOUR ENTERPRISE.

E-GOVERNMENT 2.0

n. Using modern technologies to improve government transparency, engagement, and services. Commonly employed by public sector IT, policymakers, and civic tech enthusiasts.

"E-Government 2.0 promised to modernize public services, but so far it's just a better way to send auto-replies."

Related Terms: Digital transformation, Citizen feedback, Public policy

E-GOVERNMENT PLATFORMS

n. Digital platforms providing online government services. Commonly employed by government agencies modernizing public services.

"Our E-Government platform turned paying taxes into a thrilling online scavenger hunt—just kidding, it's still awful."

Related Terms: E-Government 2.0, Census data, Transparency

E-COMMERCE

n. Buying and selling goods or services over the internet. Commonly employed by retailers, entrepreneurs, and digital marketers.

"Our e-commerce site sold five items this quarter, which is better than zero if you love small victories."

Related Terms: Conversion rate, Cloud computing, Cross-channel marketing

E-GOVERNMENT

n. The use of digital technologies by government to provide services and interact with citizens. Commonly employed by policymakers, IT in public sector, and civic engagement groups.

"E-government let citizens file complaints online, ensuring they could be ignored digitally instead of in person."

Related Terms: E-Government 2.0, E-Government platforms, Digital divide

EA (EXECUTIVE ASSISTANT)

n. Someone who supports senior-level managers or executives, handling schedules, communications, and logistics. Commonly employed by executives, HR, and administrative services.

"Our EA schedules meetings so precisely that the CEO can micromanage in five-minute increments."

Related Terms: Chair, Facipulate, DNB (Do Not Bother/Book)

EDM (ELECTRONIC DIRECT MAIL MARKETING)

n. Email marketing campaigns targeting customers directly. Commonly employed by marketers, email strategists, and sales teams.

"Our EDM campaigns are so captivating that customers mark them as spam just to save the good stuff for later—sure, we'll believe that."

Related Terms: A/B testing, Conversion rate, Contextual targeting

EOD (END OF DAY)

abbr. Typically the end of the workday, often considered 5:00 PM. Commonly employed by managers, colleagues, and clients setting short deadlines.

"When they say 'send it by EOD,' they mean do it at 4:59 PM and pray your inbox doesn't explode."

Related Terms: EOD/EOW, ASAP (As Soon As Possible), Cadence

EOD/EOW

abbr. End of Day (EOD) or End of Week (EOW), indicating deadlines. Commonly employed by managers, PMs, and clients specifying timeframes.

"I have 15 tasks due EOD/EOW, which is corporate code for 'expect a breakdown by Thursday.'"

Related Terms: EOD (End Of Day), ASAP (As Soon As Possible), DNB (Do Not Bother/Book)

EOM (END OF MESSAGE)

abbr. Used in emails to signal the subject line contains the entire message. Commonly employed by senders aiming for quick communication without body text.

"We used EOM so often that reading the subject line was more thrilling than the empty email body."

Related Terms: FYI (For Your Information), EDM (Electronic Direct Mail Marketing), ASAP (As Soon As Possible)

ETA (ESTIMATED TIME OF ARRIVAL)

n. When something or someone is expected to arrive or be completed. Commonly employed by managers, team leads, and clients checking on progress.

"'What's the ETA?' asked the manager, as if deadlines are more than optimistic guesses written in invisible ink."

Related Terms: EOD (End Of Day), EOD/EOW, Cadence

ECONOMIC STIMULUS

n. Government measures to boost economic activity during a downturn. Commonly employed by policymakers, economists, and commentators discussing fiscal policy.

"Our 'economic stimulus' felt like handing out coupons after the store burned down."

Related Terms: Debt ceiling, Fiscal policy, Public policy

ECOSYSTEM

n. A network of interrelated businesses, technologies, or stakeholders supporting a market. Commonly employed by strategists, investors, and entrepreneurs describing industry structures.

"Our tech ecosystem is a jungle where startups swing from funding rounds to bankruptcies in record time."

Related Terms: E-commerce, Innovation, Digital transformation

ELECTION INTEGRITY

n. Ensuring elections are free, fair, and transparent. Commonly employed by policymakers, election officials, and watchdog groups.

"We cared about election integrity, or at least we said so really loudly every time a camera was near."

Related Terms: Elections commission, Public policy, Governmental transparency

ELECTIONS COMMISSION

n. A government body overseeing electoral processes and ensuring fairness. Commonly employed by governments, political parties, and international observers.

"The elections commission demanded fairness, so we gave them a front-row seat to our three-ring circus of confusion."

Related Terms: Election integrity, Public policy, Chatham House Rules

ELECTRONIC HEALTH RECORD (EHR)

n. A digital version of a patient's paper chart, storing medical history electronically. Commonly employed by healthcare providers, hospitals, and clinics improving record-keeping.

"Our EHR system was so secure and user-friendly that doctors needed a Ouija board to access patient info."

Related Terms: Care coordination, Chronic care management, Value-based care

ELEPHANT IN THE ROOM

n. An obvious issue or problem people are reluctant to discuss. Commonly employed by managers, team members, and consultants acknowledging ignored conflicts.

"The elephant in the room was the CEO's endless babbling, which we pretended was strategic insight."

Related Terms: Bubble mentality, Canary in the coal mine

ELEVATOR PITCH

n. A concise summary of an idea, product, or service, quick enough to deliver in an elevator ride. Commonly employed by entrepreneurs, sales reps, and job seekers.

"My elevator pitch ended right when the CFO asked, 'So what's the point?'—timing is everything."

Related Terms: Pitch deck, Go to market, Value proposition

ELITISM

n. The belief that certain individuals or groups are superior and deserve special treatment. Commonly employed by critics describing snobbery in corporate boards or leadership.

"Our board's elitism showed when they suggested employees dine on caviar as a morale booster."

Related Terms: Empty suit, Culture fit, Bubble mentality

EMERGENCY MEDICAL SERVICES (EMS)

n. Urgent medical care and ambulance transport for emergencies. Commonly employed by healthcare systems, hospitals, and first responders.

"We joked about calling EMS during the budget meeting, as our hopes flatlined halfway through."

Related Terms: Critical care, Care coordination, Value-based care

EMPOWER

v. To give someone authority, resources, or confidence to succeed. Commonly employed by managers, HR, and leadership encouraging autonomy.

"They said they'd empower us, but all we got was a motivational poster and a broken stapler."

Related Terms: Champion, Change management, Aces in their places

EMPTY CALORIES

n. Activities consuming time without producing meaningful results. Commonly employed by employees and critics of pointless tasks.

"Half of our weekly tasks are empty calories—filling us with pointless busywork until we can't taste productivity anymore."

Related Terms: Busy work, Donkey work, Flogging a dead horse

EMPTY SUIT

n. A person in authority who lacks real skills, influence, or substance. Commonly employed by employees mocking ineffective executives or managers.

"Our VP was an empty suit, impressing no one except the mirror he consulted hourly."

Related Terms: Elitism, HiPPO (Highest-Paid Person's Opinion), Above my paygrade

END-OF-LIFE CARE

n. Healthcare focusing on comfort rather than cure for individuals nearing the end of life. Commonly employed by hospice, palliative care, and medical providers.

"We gave the failing project end-of-life care, which meant quietly pulling the plug and sending a memo about 'reallocation.'"

Related Terms: Critical care, Chronic care management, Value-based care

ENDOWMENT FUND

n. A fund established for ongoing financial support, often invested long-term by nonprofits or institutions. Commonly employed by universities, foundations, and charities.

"Our endowment fund's growth rate resembled a snail's pace—if that snail had a limp."

Related Terms: 501(c)(3), Capital campaign, Charitable giving

ENGAGE

v. To involve or collaborate with others actively and meaningfully. Commonly employed by facilitators, leaders, and community managers.

"When they told us to engage, we asked if that meant actual dialogue or another Zoom call of muted head-nodding."

Related Terms: Facipulate, Consensus building, Stakeholder engagement

ENVIRONMENTAL IMPACT ASSESSMENT (EIA)

n. Evaluating the environmental effects of a proposed project before decisions are made. Commonly employed by policymakers, environmental consultants, and planners.

"Our EIA showed building a factory on a penguin sanctuary was 'frowned upon,' who could've guessed?"

Related Terms: Carbon pricing, Sustainability, Regulatory compliance

EQUITY

n. The difference between an asset's market value and what's owed on it; also fairness or ownership. Commonly employed by investors, homeowners, and companies discussing share ownership.

"We bragged about equity until the market crashed and we realized we were rich only in regret."

Related Terms: 1031 exchange, Cap rate (Capitalization rate), Real estate investment concepts if any: Investment property

ESCROW

n. A neutral third-party account holding funds until conditions are met. Commonly employed by real estate agents, attorneys, and buyers/sellers ensuring trust in transactions.

"Our home sale got stuck in escrow so long we decorated the paperwork for the holidays."

Related Terms: 1031 exchange, Real estate closing, Cap rate (Capitalization rate)

EXECUTIVE DECISION

n. A decision made by a leader or executive without group input. Commonly employed by top management asserting authority.

"Our CEO made an executive decision to rebrand after watching a TikTok—truly data-driven leadership."

Related Terms: HiPPO (Highest-Paid Person's Opinion), Above my paygrade, Change management

EXECUTIVE SUMMARY

n. A concise overview of key information, often at the start of a report. Commonly employed by analysts, consultants, and project leads to highlight main points.

"Our executive summary was so concise it basically said 'We tried, sorry!' in three bullet points."

Related Terms: Due diligence, Cost-benefit analysis, Business case

EXIT STRATEGY

n. A plan for how an investor or entrepreneur will realize returns and depart an investment. Commonly employed by startup founders, investors, and business owners.

"Our exit strategy involved the founders disappearing into the night before anyone asked for refunds."

Related Terms: Burning bridges, VC (Venture Capital), Go to market

F
IS FOR FREEMIUM BECAUSE FREEMIUM FEATURES FOOL FOLKS INTO FINDING FUN, FINALLY FORCING THEM TO FUND YOUR FUTURE.

F2F (FACE-TO-FACE)

abbr. Meeting or interacting in person rather than virtually. Commonly employed by managers, HR, and teams emphasizing personal interaction.

"We requested an F2F meeting, but management said Zoom filters were cheaper than real human interaction."

Related Terms: Engage, Facipulate, Face time

FOMO (FEAR OF MISSING OUT)

abbr. Anxiety that one is missing a valuable experience, driving impulsive decisions. Commonly employed by marketers, event organizers, and product launches using scarcity tactics.

"We launched a limited-time offer to exploit customers' FOMO, turning mild interest into panicked clicking."

Related Terms: Crowdfunding, ASAP (As Soon As Possible), Conversion rate

FTE (FULL-TIME EMPLOYEE)

abbr. A staff member working the standard full-time hours. Commonly employed by HR, finance, and management counting workforce capacity.

"Our FTE count dropped when interns fled to actual careers with fewer 'mandatory fun' sessions."

Related Terms: Culture fit, Aces in their places, Burnout

FYI (FOR YOUR INFORMATION)

abbr. Sharing information without requiring action. Commonly employed by colleagues, managers, and team members keeping others informed.

"I sent an FYI email at 6 PM Friday, basically saying 'Happy weekend, here's more anxiety fodder.'"

Related Terms: EOM (End Of Message), ASAP (As Soon As Possible), DNB (Do Not Bother/Book)

FACE TIME

n. Opportunities for direct, in-person interaction or discussion. Commonly employed by managers, leaders, and teams valuing personal connection.

"We scheduled face time with the boss, which basically meant smiling at his monologue and nodding until we forgot our own names."

Related Terms: F2F (Face-to-Face), Engage, Facipulate

FACIPULATE (FACILITATE + MANIPULATE)

v. Guiding others while secretly steering the outcome, i.e., facilitating with an agenda. Commonly employed by clever managers or consultants pushing a preferred solution.

"Our manager tried to facipulate the brainstorming session, steering us toward his pet idea like a puppeteer."

Related Terms: Consensus building, Chair, Chatham House Rules

FACT PATTERN

n. A collection of evidence or details supporting a position or argument. Commonly employed by lawyers, analysts, and investigators.

"We assembled a fact pattern to prove we were right, then realized facts have no power in a land of opinions and gut feelings."

Related Terms: Due diligence, Case study, Deep dive

FACTORY FLOOR CHAOS

n. Disorganized, miscommunicated conditions in a manufacturing environment. Commonly employed by operations managers, safety inspectors, and labor groups.

"The factory floor chaos made it look like we'd given toddlers power tools and said, 'Go forth and manufacture, kiddos.'"

Related Terms: Broken workflow, Bottleneck, Process fatigue

FAILOVER FAILURE

n. When backup systems fail during emergencies, nullifying contingency plans. Commonly employed by IT, disaster recovery teams, and operational managers.

"Our failover failure was so spectacular that the backup plan waved a white flag before collapsing into shame."

Related Terms: Crisis management, Fire drill, Risk management

FAIRY DUST

n. Minor adjustments or refinements made at the end of a project, often cosmetic. Commonly employed sarcastically by teams trying to polish a flawed result.

"We sprinkled fairy dust on the final report, hoping a few pretty charts would hide the gaping logical holes."

Related Terms: Busy work, Donkey work, Flogging a dead horse

FAKER'S DOZEN

n. Repeatedly calling out sick or frequently absent without real cause. Commonly employed by managers and HR noting suspicious employee attendance.

"Bob took a faker's dozen of sick days this month—apparently, being allergic to Mondays is a real condition now."

Related Terms: Dead weight, Busy work, FTE (Full-Time Employee)

FALL GUY

n. Someone designated to take the blame for problems caused by others. Commonly employed by teams, managers, or executives seeking scapegoats.

"After the project bombed, we needed a fall guy—guess who got voluntold? The intern who once asked for a raise."

Related Terms: CYA (Cover Your Ass), Above my paygrade, Burning bridges

FALLEN ANGELS

n. Investments once high-performing but now significantly declined in value. Commonly employed by investors, analysts, and portfolio managers.

"Our 'fallen angels' portfolio looked like a stock graveyard where good returns went to die."

Related Terms: Death spiral, Depreciation, Cap rate (Capitalization rate)

FAT FINGER ERROR

n. A mistake caused by pressing the wrong button or key, often in financial transactions. Commonly employed by traders, IT staff, and analysts referencing input blunders.

"One fat finger error and we accidentally bought 10,000 shares of a failing snail farm."

Related Terms: Drop the ball, Crisis mode, Due diligence

FEE-FOR-SERVICE

n. A healthcare payment model paying providers for each service rendered. Commonly employed by insurers, healthcare administrators, and policy analysts.

"Under fee-for-service, the doctor billed me for breathing too loudly in the waiting room—talk about thoroughness."

Related Terms: Value-based care, Capitation, Bundled payments

FEEDING THE BEAST

phrase. Continually providing resources to a process or project yielding little value. Commonly employed by managers, teams, or critics of endless busywork.

"We kept feeding the beast of bureaucracy, hoping one day it would burp out progress instead of devouring our souls."

Related Terms: Busy work, Bureaucratic red tape, Flogging a dead horse

FINTECH (FINANCIAL TECHNOLOGY)

n. Technology applied to improve and automate financial services. Commonly employed by startups, banks, and innovators disrupting traditional finance.

"Our FinTech startup promised to 'revolutionize banking,' which meant turning loan approvals into a confusing app."

Related Terms: DeFi (Decentralized Finance), Fintech unicorn, Crypto wallet

FINANCIAL TRANSPARENCY

n. Openly sharing financial information with stakeholders for trust and accountability. Commonly employed by CFOs, auditors, and regulators encouraging honest reporting.

"Our version of financial transparency is a pie chart that says 'Trust Us' in 72-point font."

Related Terms: Due diligence, Regulatory compliance, Governmental transparency

FINTECH UNICORN

n. A fintech startup valued at over $1 billion. Commonly employed by investors, media, and entrepreneurs admiring rare success stories.

"We dreamed of becoming a fintech unicorn, but our valuation barely hit 'fintech donkey.'"

Related Terms: FinTech (Financial Technology), VC (Venture Capital), Disruption

FIRE DRILL

n. An unplanned event or task requiring immediate attention, analogous to an emergency test. Commonly employed by managers and teams suddenly rushing to fix urgent issues.

"They called it a 'fire drill,' but it felt more like 'We forgot to plan, so scramble, minions!'"

Related Terms: Crisis management, Failover failure, Crisis mode

FIREFIGHTING

n. Constantly reacting to crises rather than preventing them. Commonly employed by teams stuck in reactive modes, lacking long-term strategy.

"Our day-to-day is firefighting; we'd invest in prevention, but who has time when everything's always on fire?"

Related Terms: Crisis mode, Don't boil the ocean, Death by a thousand cuts

FIRST PASS/QUICK PASS

n. An initial, cursory review or draft before more detailed work. Commonly employed by editors, managers, and team leads for early feedback.

"My first pass at the report was so rough it made sandpaper look silky."

Related Terms: Deep dive, Brain dump, Drill down

FIRST-PARTY DATA

n. Data collected directly from a company's own audience or customers. Commonly employed by marketers, data analysts, and product teams seeking reliable insights.

"Our first-party data revealed customers hate our pop-up ads—shocking news that required no data to guess."

Related Terms: Cookie tracking, DMP (Data management platform), A/B testing

FISCAL POLICY

n. Government policies related to taxation, spending, and budgeting. Commonly employed by economists, policymakers, and analysts discussing macroeconomic strategies.

"Our fiscal policy in the office is to tax positive attitudes and spend lavishly on coffee creamer."

Related Terms: Economic stimulus, Debt ceiling, Public policy

FISCAL RESPONSIBILITY

n. Managing spending, budgeting, and debt to promote stability. Commonly employed by policymakers, CFOs, and executives stressing prudence.

"Our idea of fiscal responsibility was not buying the gold-plated stapler, but a silver one—truly heroic restraint."

Related Terms: Fiscal policy, Cost-benefit analysis, Governmental transparency

FIXED-RATE MORTGAGE

n. A mortgage with a constant interest rate for the entire loan term. Commonly employed by homebuyers and lenders preferring predictable payments.

"With a fixed-rate mortgage, at least the bank's monthly insult to my wallet is reliably consistent."

Related Terms: Foreclosure, Real estate closing, 1031 exchange

FLAG

v. To highlight or draw attention to an issue or topic. Commonly employed by analysts, QA testers, and team leads noting problems.

"I flagged the budget discrepancy, and the CFO thanked me by promoting me to Chief 'Stop Ruining My Day' Officer."

Related Terms: Good catch, Risk management, Due diligence

FLESH OUT

v. Adding details or context to clarify a subject. Commonly employed by writers, PMs, and stakeholders refining plans.

"We tried to flesh out the proposal, but it went from 'vague idea' to 'rambling manifesto' in minutes."

Related Terms: Deep dive, First pass/quick pass, Drill down

FLOGGING A DEAD HORSE

phrase. Investing effort in something that cannot succeed. Commonly employed by teams, employees, or managers describing futile persistence.

"Revisiting that old marketing plan is like flogging a dead horse—except the horse had more potential."

Related Terms: Can of worms, Feeding the beast, Busy work

FLOUNDERING

v. Struggling or failing to make progress. Commonly employed by managers and observers describing teams stuck in confusion.

"Our team's strategy meeting was floundering, like a fish gasping on dry land while we applauded its effort."

Related Terms: Broken workflow, Scope creep, Death march

FLUFF

n. Superficial or unnecessary content adding no real value. Commonly employed by critics of reports, presentations, or marketing material.

"The report was 90% fluff—fancy words adding about as much value as confetti at a funeral."

Related Terms: Bullshit bingo, Management speak, Cookie-cutter approach

FLY-BY-NIGHT

n. Unreliable or short-lived operations likely to fail quickly. Commonly employed by critics describing vendors or businesses that disappear without a trace.

"Our vendor was so fly-by-night that their contract ended before we learned their CEO's last name."

Related Terms: Bottom feeder, Death spiral, Dumpster fire

FORECLOSURE

n. The legal process where a lender takes ownership of a property after the owner fails to pay. Commonly employed by banks, mortgage lenders, and courts in real estate finance.

"The bank's foreclosure on our investment property was the final punchline in our comedy of errors."

Related Terms: Fixed-rate mortgage, Real estate closing, 1031 exchange

FOREIGN AID

n. Assistance provided by one country to another, often for development or relief. Commonly employed by governments, NGOs, and international organizations.

"Our office's version of foreign aid was lending the neighboring department a stapler and a pitying glance."

Related Terms: Public policy, Economic stimulus, Community outreach

FRAMEWORK

n. A structured approach or method guiding tasks or objectives. Commonly employed by consultants, strategists, and PMs providing structure to projects.

"We built a framework for success so flexible it bent under the weight of our own confusion."

Related Terms: Matrices, Granular, Cookie-cutter approach

FRANCHISE TAX

n. A tax imposed on businesses for the privilege of operating in a certain area. Commonly employed by states, local governments, and tax authorities.

"Paying franchise tax felt like a cover charge to enter a party where the music is bad and drinks are expensive."

Related Terms: Fiscal policy, Corporate tax rate, Regulatory compliance

FREEDOM OF INFORMATION ACT (FOIA)

n. A law ensuring public access to certain government records. Commonly employed by journalists, activists, and watchdogs seeking transparency.

"We filed a FOIA request hoping for transparency and got 1,000 pages of redacted glory— like a spy novel without the plot."

Related Terms: Governmental transparency, Chatham House Rules, Public policy

FREEDOM OF SPEECH

n. The right to publicly express opinions without government interference. Commonly employed by citizens, media, and activists in democratic societies.

"In our meetings, freedom of speech means you can complain all you want, as long as you agree with the boss."

Related Terms: Election integrity, Civil liberties, Chatham House Rules

FREEMIUM

n. Offering basic services for free while charging for premium features. Commonly employed by software developers, app creators, and online services.

"Our freemium model let customers taste disappointment for free, then pay to upgrade their disappointment."

Related Terms: Freemium model, SaaS (Software as a Service), Conversion rate

FREEMIUM MODEL

n. The same as freemium, where a basic version is free and advanced features cost extra. Commonly employed by startups, SaaS companies, and digital product teams.

"We adopted a freemium model so users could feel cheap and desperate before finally opening their wallets."

Related Terms: Freemium, A/B testing, Client-centric

FUNCTION VS. INDUSTRY

n. Distinguishing roles by their department (function) versus their broader field (industry). Commonly employed by org designers, HR, and analysts clarifying org structures.

"In our org chart, function vs. industry debates were as useful as arguing whether the Titanic sank horizontally or vertically."

Related Terms: Dotted line vs. Solid line (reporting), Aces in their places, Culture fit

FUNDRAISING APPEAL

n. A request for donations to support a nonprofit cause or initiative. Commonly employed by nonprofits, charities, and fundraising professionals.

"Our fundraising appeal read like a ransom note, demanding money for 'urgent missions' no one understood."

Related Terms: Fundraising campaign, Donor stewardship, Capital campaign

FUNDRAISING CAMPAIGN

n. A structured effort to raise money for a specific cause or project. Commonly employed by nonprofits, charities, and political groups.

"Our fundraising campaign tried emotional pleas, guilt-trips, and catchy jingles—turns out people are immune to all three."

Related Terms: Fundraising appeal, Capital campaign, Charitable giving

FUNDRAISING EVENT

n. A special occasion organized to raise money for a cause. Commonly employed by nonprofits, schools, and charities seeking direct community support.

"At our fundraising event, guests paid for overpriced hors d'oeuvres and a silent auction of things no one needed."

Related Terms: Fundraising campaign, Donor recognition, Community outreach

G

IS FOR GO-TO-MARKET STRATEGY BECAUSE GAINING GROUND GLOBALLY GROWS GROSS GAINS —GET GOING, GOOD LUCK, AND GO-TO-MARKET NOW.

GAIN TRACTION

v. Making progress or gathering momentum on a project, product, or initiative. Commonly employed by startups, product teams, and marketers tracking progress.

"Our marketing plan finally gained traction after we stopped acting like clowns juggling buzzwords in the dark."

Related Terms: Go-to-market strategy, Buy-in, Conversion rate

GAME CHANGER

n. Something that significantly alters a company's operations, strategy, or market. Commonly employed by execs, investors, and innovators applauding major shifts.

"They called it a game changer, but it felt more like changing Monopoly to a game where nobody wins and the bank is always broke."

Related Terms: Disruptive, Innovation, Go to market

GANTT CHART

n. A visual timeline showing tasks, deadlines, and progress in project management. Commonly employed by project managers and planners tracking schedules.

"We updated the Gantt chart so frequently it became our version of reality TV—just with fewer redeeming qualities."

Related Terms: Critical path, Deliverables, Scope

GEO-FENCING

n. Using location-based technology to trigger actions, like notifications, when entering a defined area. Commonly employed by marketers, event organizers, and security firms.

"We geo-fenced the office, so employees got reminders to be 'productive' the moment they stepped inside—big brother approves."

Related Terms: Geotargeting, Contextual targeting, Cross-channel marketing

GEOTARGETING

n. Delivering ads or content based on a user's geographic location. Commonly employed by marketers, advertisers, and localization teams.

"Our geotargeting showed ads for winter coats to people in Florida, proving the algorithm was drunk again."

Related Terms: Geo-fencing, Contextual targeting, A/B testing

GET THE BALL ROLLING

phrase. To initiate or start a project, task, or discussion. Commonly employed by leaders, colleagues, and facilitators encouraging quick starts.

"We got the ball rolling on the new initiative right before tripping over it and sending it off a cliff."

Related Terms: Dive right in, Brain dump, Cadence

GIVE A HEADS UP

phrase. To warn or inform someone ahead of an action or event. Commonly employed by managers, teammates, and friends to prevent surprises.

"They gave me a heads up about the new policy, which arrived exactly two minutes before it ruined my afternoon."

Related Terms: FYI (For Your Information), EOM (End Of Message), Chime in

GIVING 110%

phrase. Putting in extra effort beyond what's typical or expected. Commonly employed by motivational speakers, managers, and coaches.

"Our manager demands we give 110%, as if math and basic realism don't apply in this office."

Related Terms: Burnout, Aces in their places, Go to market

GLASS CEILING

n. An invisible barrier preventing certain groups from advancing to higher levels. Commonly employed by diversity advocates, HR, and career counselors.

"She hit the glass ceiling so hard she considered bringing a sledgehammer to the next board meeting."

Related Terms: Culture fit, Elitism, Above my paygrade

GO TO MARKET

phrase. A plan or strategy for introducing a product or service to the market. Commonly employed by product managers, marketers, and sales teams launching offerings.

"Our go-to-market strategy involved wishful thinking and a few catchy slogans, because who needs research?"

Related Terms: Go-to-market strategy, Game changer, Innovation

GO-TO-MARKET STRATEGY

n. The detailed approach a company takes to sell and deliver its products to customers. Commonly employed by product leads, marketers, and executives planning launches.

"Our go-to-market strategy was so vague it might as well have been a treasure map drawn by a blind pirate."

Related Terms: Go to market, A/B testing, Gain traction

GOING FORWARD

phrase. Actions or plans taken from this point onward. Commonly employed by managers, execs, and project leads focusing on the future.

"Going forward, we'll pretend this quarter never happened and hope no one remembers the dumpster fire."

Related Terms: Change management, Digital transformation, Consensus building

GOLDEN HANDCUFFS

n. Financial incentives that make it difficult or undesirable for an employee to leave a company. Commonly employed by HR, CFOs, and executives retaining key talent.

"The golden handcuffs kept our star developer from quitting, but didn't stop him from glaring at us every morning."

Related Terms: FTE (Full-Time Employee), Burnout, Aces in their places

GOOD CATCH

phrase. Acknowledging when someone notices an error or issue, often with gratitude. Commonly employed by managers, teammates, and editors encouraging attention to detail.

"'Good catch,' said the boss, as if noticing a glaring mistake was a heroic feat instead of basic competence."

Related Terms: Flag, Due diligence, CYA (Cover Your Ass)

GOVERNMENT ACCOUNTABILITY

n. The obligation of government officials to answer for their actions and decisions. Commonly employed by watchdogs, citizens, and NGOs demanding transparency.

"Government accountability meant we got a 300-page report explaining nothing, but hey, it sure looked official."

Related Terms: FOIA (Freedom of information act), Governmental transparency, Election integrity

GOVERNMENT ACCOUNTABILITY OFFICE (GAO)

n. An independent U.S. agency auditing and evaluating government programs. Commonly employed by policymakers, taxpayers, and oversight committees.

"The GAO told us our spending was 'problematic,' which is bureaucratic for 'Who taught you to budget—an intoxicated raccoon?'"

Related Terms: Government accountability, Public policy, Fiscal responsibility

GOVERNMENT BAILOUTS

n. Financial assistance provided by the government to struggling entities. Commonly employed by analysts, citizens, and policymakers debating rescue measures.

"We waited for government bailouts like kids waiting for Santa, except Santa charged interest and asked for votes."

Related Terms: Economic stimulus, Fiscal policy, Corporate welfare

GOVERNMENT PRIVATIZATION

n. Transferring government services or assets to the private sector. Commonly employed by policymakers, economists, and critics debating efficiency vs. public interest.

"After government privatization, our public library got replaced by a vending machine charging $5 per page."

Related Terms: Public policy, Fiscal policy, Regulatory compliance

GOVERNMENT PROCUREMENT

n. The process by which government agencies acquire goods, services, or works. Commonly employed by public sector buyers, vendors, and compliance officers.

"Our government procurement process makes buying paper clips feel like negotiating a nuclear arms treaty." Related Terms: Bureaucratic red tape, Fiscal responsibility, Government accountability

GOVERNMENT SHUTDOWN

n. The closure of government agencies due to failure to pass funding bills. Commonly employed by media, citizens, and policymakers during budget impasses.

"During the government shutdown, we realized that no one noticed the difference—sadly telling."

Related Terms: Debt ceiling, Fiscal policy, Economic stimulus

GOVERNMENTAL TRANSPARENCY

n. Openness of government actions, decisions, and policies to public scrutiny. Commonly employed by activists, journalists, and good governance advocates.

"Our government's idea of transparency is releasing reports so redacted they look like zebra stripes."

Related Terms: FOIA (Freedom of information act), Election integrity, Government accountability

GRANDFATHERING

n. Allowing existing participants or conditions to continue under old rules while new ones follow updated regulations. Commonly employed by policymakers, HR, and legal teams managing transitions.

"We grandfathered the old users in, ensuring they can enjoy outdated chaos while newcomers face shiny new confusion."

Related Terms: Change management, Regulatory compliance, Scope creep

GRANT CYCLE

n. The process through which grant applications are solicited, reviewed, and awarded. Commonly employed by nonprofits, foundations, and grantmakers.

"Our grant cycle felt like waiting for a miracle, except with more paperwork and fewer actual miracles."

Related Terms: Fundraising campaign, Donor stewardship, Capital campaign

GRANT FUNDING

n. Financial aid given by an organization without requiring repayment. Commonly employed by nonprofits, researchers, and educational institutions.

"We got grant funding to study snail migration, because apparently no cause is too obscure."

Related Terms: Grant cycle, Donor advised fund (DAF), Charitable giving

GRANT WRITING

n. The process of writing proposals to secure grants or funding. Commonly employed by nonprofits, researchers, and fundraisers.

"Grant writing is like begging politely on paper, hoping someone's too bored to reject you."

Related Terms: Grant funding, Fundraising appeal, Due diligence

GRANULAR

adj. Focusing on small, detailed components rather than the big picture. Commonly employed by analysts, project leads, and data specialists.

"Our manager got so granular we spent an hour debating the font size on a footnote no one would read."

Related Terms: Flesh out, Matrices, Deep dive

GRAVEYARD SHIFT

n. Working late-night hours when most people are asleep. Commonly employed by 24/7 businesses, factories, and healthcare services.

"On the graveyard shift, even spreadsheets look haunted and coffee tastes like surrender."

Related Terms: Burnout, Donkey work, Busy work

GREEN

adj. Inexperienced or new to a field. Commonly employed by managers, mentors, and HR noting a newcomer's lack of experience.

"Our new hire was so green that he asked if synergy was a type of yoga pose."

Related Terms: Aces in their places, Culture fit, Skillset

GREEN BUILDING

n. Environmentally responsible and resource-efficient construction practices. Commonly employed by architects, developers, and sustainability advocates.

"We called it a green building because the paint was eco-friendly, ignoring the HVAC screamed like a dying whale."

Related Terms: EIA (Environmental impact assessment), Sustainability, Carbon pricing

GREENFIELD SITE

n. Undeveloped land used for new projects or construction. Commonly employed by real estate developers, urban planners, and investors.

"Developing a greenfield site sounded fun until we realized 'undeveloped' meant 'enjoy the weeds and rodent families.'"

Related Terms: Brownfield site, Real estate development, Cap rate (Capitalization rate)

GROUNDHOG DAY

n. Experiencing repetitive cycles where the same issues recur over and over. Commonly employed by employees stuck in loops of pointless meetings.

"Our weekly status meeting was Groundhog Day: same agenda, same excuses, different plaid shirt."

Related Terms: Broken record, In the weeds, Flogging a dead horse

GROWTH HACKING

n. Rapid, low-cost marketing strategies aimed at quick growth in user base or revenue. Commonly employed by startups, marketers, and product teams seeking explosive expansion.

"We tried growth hacking, which involved more hack than growth, and a side of desperate tweeting."

Related Terms: A/B testing, Gain traction, Freemium

GUT FEEL

n. An immediate, instinctive reaction not based on data or analysis. Commonly employed by managers, leaders, and old-school decision-makers relying on intuition.

"We relied on gut feel instead of research, like throwing darts blindfolded and calling it strategy."

Related Terms: HiPPO (Highest-Paid Person's Opinion), Bubble mentality, Drink the Kool-Aid

H

IS FOR HELICOPTER MANAGER BECAUSE HOVERING HELICOPTER MANAGERS HINDER HARMONIOUS HAPPENINGS— HALT THE HOVERING!

HMO (HEALTH MAINTENANCE ORGANIZATION)

abbr. + n. A health insurance plan requiring members to use doctors within a network. Commonly employed by insurers, healthcare administrators, and patients seeking lower-cost care.

"My HMO provided so little choice that picking a doctor felt like choosing from a menu of stale crackers."

Related Terms: Capitation, Value-based care, Chronic care management

HR (HUMAN RESOURCES)

abbr. + n. The department handling staffing, benefits, and workplace issues. Commonly employed by companies of all sizes to manage employee relations.

"Our HR team excelled at handing out policy memos and awkward smiles, which is a talent, I guess."

Related Terms: Culture fit, Aces in their places, Golden handcuffs

HARD COPY

n. A printed, physical version of a document. Commonly employed by managers, legal teams, and auditors preferring tangible records.

"The boss demanded a hard copy, presumably to reminisce about the Stone Age of business documentation."

Related Terms: Deliverable, Paper shredder, CYA (Cover Your Ass)

HARD STOP

n. A fixed end time for a meeting or discussion, after which no extension is allowed. Commonly employed by busy executives, managers, or anyone with tight schedules.

"We have a hard stop at 5 PM, so naturally the CEO arrived at 4:59 with a slideshow called 'Overtime Ideas.'"

Related Terms: Cadence, DNB (Do Not Bother/Book), EOD (End Of Day)

HAS LEGS

phrase. A concept or initiative with potential for long-term success. Commonly employed by venture capitalists, product leads, and strategists evaluating ideas.

"Our pitch 'has legs,' said the director, as if it weren't limping into mediocrity at best."

Related Terms: Gain traction, Game changer, Go-to-market strategy

HEADS DOWN

adj. Working with focused concentration, avoiding distractions. Commonly employed by team leads and managers encouraging quiet productivity.

"We went heads down on the project, which meant minimal eye contact, zero laughter, and the ambiance of a funeral home."

Related Terms: Timebox, In the weeds, Burnout

HEADWINDS VS. TAILWINDS

n. Headwinds are challenges slowing progress; tailwinds are favorable conditions aiding it. Commonly employed by analysts, strategists, and economists describing external factors.

"We faced so many headwinds that even a rocket booster made of corporate slogans wouldn't help us take off."

Related Terms: Gain traction, Disruption, Scope creep

HEALTH INSURANCE PORTABILITY

n. The ability to maintain health coverage when changing jobs or plans. Commonly employed by HR, policymakers, and advocacy groups promoting stable coverage.

"Health insurance portability is nice in theory, like world peace or mandatory four-day weekends."

Related Terms: HMO (Health Maintenance Organization), Value-based care, Chronic care management

HEALTH RISK ASSESSMENT

n. A tool evaluating an individual's overall health to identify potential risks. Commonly employed by insurers, wellness programs, and healthcare providers.

"Our health risk assessment revealed shocking results: stress levels skyrocketing due to endless pointless meetings."

Related Terms: Care coordination, Chronic care management, Inpatient care

HEALTH SAVINGS ACCOUNT (HSA)

n. A tax-advantaged savings account for healthcare expenses. Commonly employed by employees, HR, and insurers offering flexible spending options.

"My HSA covered that hospital bill, leaving me just enough leftover to buy a bandage—thrilling."

Related Terms: Value-based care, HMO (Health Maintenance Organization), Capitation

HEALTHCARE WORKFORCE DEVELOPMENT

n. Ensuring a sufficient and skilled healthcare workforce to meet demand. Commonly employed by hospitals, policymakers, and training programs.

"Our healthcare workforce development plan: hoping nurses magically sprout from our underfunded training programs."

Related Terms: Chronic care management, Integrated care, Accountable care organization (ACO)

HELICOPTER MANAGER

n. A manager who hovers excessively, micromanaging every detail. Commonly employed by employees describing overbearing bosses.

"Our helicopter manager monitored our keystrokes so closely I wondered if she believed we typed in Morse code."

Related Terms: Facipulate, HiPPO (Highest-Paid Person's Opinion), In the weeds

HERDING CATS

phrase. Attempting to manage or direct a group inherently difficult to organize. Commonly employed by project leads, managers, and anyone facing uncooperative teams.

"Convincing our creative team to agree on anything is like herding cats with commitment issues."

Related Terms: Herding turtles, Consensus building, Bubble mentality

HERDING TURTLES

phrase. Similar to herding cats, but even slower and more frustrating. Commonly employed humorously when progress is painfully sluggish.

"Our attempt to implement process improvements was like herding turtles—if the turtles had lawyers and bad attitudes."

Related Terms: Herding cats, Groundhog Day, Death march

HIPPO (HIGHEST-PAID PERSON'S OPINION)

abbr. + n. Decisions dominated by the viewpoint of the highest-paid individual, ignoring data. Commonly employed by analysts, employees, and consultants critiquing top-down authority.

"We followed the HiPPO's directive and ignored the data, because who needs facts when a big paycheck says otherwise?"

Related Terms: Gut feel, Empty suit, Drink the Kool-Aid

HIGH LEVEL

adj. A summarized explanation focusing on major points rather than details. Commonly employed by executives, speakers, and managers avoiding complexity.

"The VP gave a high-level overview that soared so far above ground we needed binoculars and oxygen masks."

Related Terms: 30,000-feet view, Holistic approach, Mission statement

HIT THE GROUND RUNNING

phrase. To begin a project or task immediately with full effort. Commonly employed by managers, recruiters, and team leads encouraging quick starts.

"We were told to hit the ground running, but we tripped over vague instructions and fell flat on confusion."

Related Terms: Dive right in, Get the ball rolling, ASAP (As Soon As Possible)

HOME EQUITY LOAN

n. A loan using the equity in a home as collateral. Commonly employed by homeowners, banks, and financial advisors.

"I took out a home equity loan to fund the kitchen remodel, now my house owes my house money—neat."

Related Terms: Fixed-rate mortgage, Foreclosure, Investment property

HOME STAGING

n. Preparing a home for sale by making it appealing to potential buyers. Commonly employed by real estate agents, homeowners, and stagers.

"*After home staging, our shabby apartment looked like a Pinterest board had thrown up tasteful throw pillows.*"

Related Terms: Real estate closing, Investment property, Greenfield site

HOMEOWNER'S ASSOCIATION (HOA)

n. A private organization managing rules and common areas in a residential community. Commonly employed by homeowners, property managers, and neighborhood boards.

"*Our HOA fined me for having a garden gnome that didn't match the mandated beige aesthetic—charming.*"

Related Terms: Culture fit, Foreclosure, Greenfield site

HOSPICE CARE

n. End-of-life care focusing on comfort rather than cure. Commonly employed by healthcare providers, families, and patients needing palliative support.

"*We gave our failing product hospice care, meaning we nodded sympathetically as it sank into oblivion.*"

Related Terms: End-of-life care, Chronic care management, Critical care

HOSTAGE MENTALITY

n. Feeling trapped in a situation due to fear or lack of alternatives. Commonly employed by employees and colleagues describing toxic workplaces.

"*We stayed late out of hostage mentality, too afraid to mention that a 14-hour day might be unhealthy.*"

Related Terms: Burnout, Golden handcuffs, Culture fit

HOT DESKING

n. An office arrangement without assigned desks, employees use available workstations as needed. Commonly employed by flexible offices, co-working spaces, and cost-conscious companies.

"*Hot desking turned our office into a daily game of musical chairs, minus the fun music and with more silent resentment.*"

Related Terms: Heads down, Cadence, DNB (Do Not Bother/Book)

HYPOTHESIS

n. A testable assumption or guess based on available information. Commonly employed by researchers, analysts, and scientists.

"My hypothesis: this new product will flop harder than a beach whale once customers see the price tag."

Related Terms: A/B testing, Counterfactual, Data-driven decisions

I

IS FOR INNOVATION BECAUSE
IGNITING INGENIOUS IDEAS
INVIGORATES INDUSTRIES—
INVEST IN INNOVATION, INSPIRE
IMPACT.

ICD-10 CODES

n. A system of codes used to classify diseases and conditions for billing and data purposes in healthcare. Commonly employed by medical coders, hospitals, and insurers.

"ICD-10 codes turned my minor injury into a bureaucratic treasure hunt with no buried treasure, just bills."

Related Terms: Capitation, Care coordination, Value-based care

ICOS (INITIAL COIN OFFERINGS)

n. A cryptocurrency-based fundraising method selling new tokens for project funding. Commonly employed by blockchain startups, investors, and crypto enthusiasts.

"Our ICO promised revolutionary disruption, which apparently meant collecting investors' money and disappearing."

Related Terms: DeFi (Decentralized Finance), Crypto wallet, FinTech (Financial Technology)

ICEBREAKER

n. An activity designed to ease tension and encourage interaction at the start of an event. Commonly employed by meeting facilitators, team leads, and event organizers.

"Our icebreaker forced everyone to share 'a fun fact,' revealing that none of us have had actual fun in years."

Related Terms: Chime in, Consensus building, Brain dump

IDEATE

v. To generate ideas, typically in a collaborative setting. Commonly employed by design thinkers, R&D teams, and creative workshops.

"We tried to ideate a solution, which is corporate-speak for 'We sat around tossing buzzwords like confetti.'"

Related Terms: Brain dump, A/B testing, Flesh out

IMPACT

n. The effect or influence of an action, often focusing on measurable outcomes. Commonly employed by nonprofits, strategists, and evaluators.

"We measured our impact by how quickly we ran out of excuses for poor performance."

Related Terms: Impact report, Case study, ROI (Return on Investment)

IMPACT INVESTING

n. Investing in ventures generating social or environmental benefits alongside financial returns. Commonly employed by socially conscious investors, foundations, and ESG funds.

"We tried impact investing, hoping to save the whales and make a buck—turns out whales don't repay principal."

Related Terms: Charitable giving, Corporate social responsibility (CSR), Philanthropy

IMPACT REPORT

n. A document outlining the outcomes and effectiveness of an organization's programs or services. Commonly employed by nonprofits, CSR teams, and grant recipients.

"Our impact report was 30 pages of graphs that said, 'We tried, we really tried, please believe us.'"

Related Terms: Impact, Case study, Due diligence

IMPOSTER SYNDROME

n. Feeling like a fraud despite evidence of competence or success. Commonly employed by professionals, high achievers, and individuals in new roles.

"I presented confidently while battling imposter syndrome so fierce I expected HR to hand me a fake diploma."

Related Terms: Drink the Kool-Aid, Burnout, HiPPO (Highest-Paid Person's Opinion)

IN THE LOOP

phrase. Being kept informed about decisions or progress. Commonly employed by teams, managers, and colleagues ensuring everyone is updated.

"They promised to keep me in the loop, but the loop was apparently closed for renovations and guarded by silence."

Related Terms: FYI (For Your Information), Stakeholder engagement, Circle back

IN THE PIPELINE

phrase. Tasks or responsibilities planned for the future but not completed yet. Commonly employed by managers, sales teams, and project leads discussing upcoming work.

"We have so many projects in the pipeline it's more like a clogged drain of half-finished ideas."

Related Terms: Cadence, Go-to-market strategy, Conversion rate

IN THE WEEDS

phrase. Focusing on small details at the expense of the bigger picture. Commonly employed by supervisors or team members urging a return to broader thinking.

"We got so in the weeds that finding a leaf was more exciting than solving the actual problem."

Related Terms: Heads down, Flesh out, Silo mentality

IN YOUR WHEELHOUSE

phrase. Within one's area of expertise or strongest skill set. Commonly employed by managers, HR, and team leads allocating tasks.

"Designing that brochure was in my wheelhouse, so of course they asked me to fix the server instead."

Related Terms: Aces in their places, Core competency, Skillset

IN-KIND DONATION

n. Non-monetary contributions, such as goods or services, instead of cash. Commonly employed by nonprofits, charities, and fundraisers receiving donated resources.

"We asked for money, got old office chairs as an in-kind donation, and pondered if we could trade them for rent."

Related Terms: Charitable giving, Donor recognition, Fundraising campaign

INCENTIVIZE

v. To motivate someone with rewards or incentives. Commonly employed by managers, sales leads, and HR designing compensation packages.

"We tried to incentivize higher sales with gift cards, because nothing fuels ambition like $10 at a coffee shop."

Related Terms: Golden handcuffs, Buy-in, Culture fit

INCUBATOR

n. A program providing resources, mentorship, and sometimes funding to early-stage startups. Commonly employed by entrepreneurs, VCs, and innovation hubs nurturing new ideas.

"Our startup joined an incubator where mentors insisted they believed in us, even as we scribbled our plan on a napkin."

Related Terms: Accelerator, Seed round, Innovation

INFLUENCER MARKETING

n. Partnering with individuals who have influence over potential customers to promote products. Commonly employed by marketing teams, brands, and social media managers.

"We paid an influencer to pretend our product mattered, and she delivered a shrug in selfie form."

Related Terms: Conversion rate, Cross-channel marketing, Programmatic advertising

INHERIT

v. To assume responsibility for a task or role previously held by someone else. Commonly employed by managers, successors, and team members taking over abandoned projects.

"I inherited the mess they called a 'project plan'—it was like receiving a family heirloom that no one wanted."

Related Terms: Dead weight, Change management

INNOVATION

n. Developing new ideas, products, or methods creating additional value. Commonly employed by executives, R&D teams, and consultants championing progress.

"Our definition of innovation was slapping a '2.0' sticker on the same old product and calling it a breakthrough."

Related Terms: Disruption, Go to market, Game changer

INPATIENT CARE

n. Medical treatment requiring a patient to stay overnight in a hospital. Commonly employed by hospitals, insurers, and healthcare providers offering intensive treatment.

"My hospital stay for inpatient care felt like a vacation, if vacations came with IV drips and itemized bills."

Related Terms: Chronic care management, Care coordination, EHR (Electronic Health Record)

INSTITUTIONAL MEMORY

n. The established methods, practices, and knowledge within an organization that persist over time. Commonly employed by managers and historians of corporate culture.

"Our institutional memory was so hazy that we repeated last year's mistakes, now with more flair."

Related Terms: Mushroom principle, BAU (Business-as-usual) trap, Change management

INTEGRATED CARE

n. Coordinating different levels of healthcare to improve patient outcomes. Commonly employed by healthcare providers, systems, and reformers seeking cohesive treatment.

"Integrated care sounded great until we realized no one actually integrated anything, just slapped fancy titles on old chaos."

Related Terms: Accountable care organization (ACO), Value-based care, Care coordination

INTEGRATED DELIVERY SYSTEM (IDS)

n. A network of healthcare providers working together to offer coordinated care. Commonly employed by hospitals, insurers, and health networks aiming for seamless patient experiences.

"Our IDS was so 'coordinated' that the patient got three conflicting treatment plans and a coupon for unrelated therapy."

Related Terms: Integrated care, Care coordination, Chronic care management

INTERAGENCY COOPERATION

n. Collaboration among different government agencies for common goals. Commonly employed by policymakers, public administrators, and joint task forces.

"Our interagency cooperation resembled a three-legged race where each agency insisted on hopping in a different direction."

Related Terms: Government accountability, Public policy, Chatham House Rules

INTERGOVERNMENTAL RELATIONS

n. Interactions and collaborations between different levels of government (local, state, national). Commonly employed by policymakers, public administrators, and agencies aligning policies.

"Our intergovernmental relations meeting ended with everyone nodding politely, then ignoring each other's emails."

Related Terms: Interagency cooperation, Public sector, Government procurement

INVESTMENT PROPERTY

n. Real estate purchased mainly for earning income or capital appreciation rather than primary residence. Commonly employed by real estate investors, landlords, and property managers.

"We bought an investment property hoping for passive income, but ended up with a passive-aggressive tenant and a leaky roof."

Related Terms: Cap rate (Capitalization rate), 1031 exchange, Real estate closing

INVITE

v. To send a request for someone to attend a meeting, event, or discussion. Commonly employed by team leads, admins, and event organizers.

"I got the meeting invite at 6 AM for a 6:05 AM start—apparently, time zones and courtesy are optional."

Related Terms: Chime in, Facipulate, F2F (Face-to-Face)

IT IS WHAT IT IS

phrase. Acknowledging a reality that cannot be changed. Commonly employed by managers, colleagues, and anyone resigned to unpleasant facts.

"When asked about the budget cuts, the CFO shrugged, said 'It is what it is,' and we all contemplated our life choices."

Related Terms: Going forward, Bubble mentality, Don't boil the ocean

ITERATE

v. To refine a process or product through repeated cycles of improvement. Commonly employed by engineers, designers, and agile teams seeking continuous enhancement.

"We iterated on the design until we realized we were going in circles, improving nothing but our tolerance for tedium."

Related Terms: A/B testing, Deep dive, Go-to-market strategy

J

IS FOR JUMPSTART BECAUSE JOLTING YOUR JOURNEY WITH A JUMPSTART JUSTIFIES JETTISONING JUNK—JAZZ UP YOUR TRAJECTORY!

JOB SECURITY THEATRE

n. Actions creating the illusion of job security without real stability. Commonly employed by employees and observers noting empty promises or superficial measures.

"Our manager held 'future planning sessions,' a form of job security theatre so transparent we could see the layoffs coming."

Related Terms: Golden handcuffs, Hostage mentality, CYA (Cover Your Ass)

JUDICIAL INDEPENDENCE

n. The principle that the judiciary should be free from political influence or pressure. Commonly employed by legal scholars, policy analysts, and governance watchdogs.

"In our office's version of judicial independence, the designated 'impartial' judge also handled payroll—coincidence, I'm sure."

Related Terms: Government accountability, Election integrity, Public policy

JUMP SHIP

phrase. To leave a company or project abruptly, often when challenges arise. Commonly employed by employees and commentators describing sudden departures.

"After the third product flop, half the marketing team decided to jump ship for a company that spelled 'success' without irony."

Related Terms: Burning bridges, Churn, Cutthroat

JUMP THE SHARK

phrase. Reaching a point where something declines in quality or relevance due to a gimmick or over-the-top action. Commonly employed by critics and insiders noting a brand or show's desperate attempts to stay interesting.

"Our app jumped the shark when we added a dancing mascot to the checkout screen—nothing says trust like random choreography."

Related Terms: Disruption, Groundhog Day, Dumpster fire

JUMPING SHIP

phrase. Another form of "jump ship," leaving a company or project under unfavorable conditions. Commonly employed by teams and HR observing a pattern of employee departures.

"We suspected employees were jumping ship when the only ones left were interns and that one loyal cactus in the corner."

Related Terms: Jump ship, Churn rate, Hostage mentality

JUMPING THE SHARK

phrase. Doing something so absurd it signals a decline or desperation. Commonly employed by critics and insiders when a show or brand loses touch with its essence.

"We tried a viral challenge featuring our CEO singing off-key, officially jumping the shark into brand embarrassment."

Related Terms: Dumpster fire, Groundhog Day, Disruption

JUMPSTART

v. To energize or initiate something quickly.

Commonly employed by managers, founders, and mentors encouraging fast beginnings.

"We tried to jumpstart the project with a motivational speech, but all we got were sleepy nods and a half-hearted golf clap."

Related Terms: Hit the ground running, Dive right in, Get the ball rolling

JUST FILLING SEATS

phrase. Referring to individuals present but contributing little of value. Commonly employed by managers, team leads, and critics of token participation.

"The board meeting was full of people just filling seats, like an audience forced to watch a very long, unfunny play."

Related Terms: Dead weight, Culture fit, Busy work

JUST-IN-CASE INVENTORY

n. Extra inventory kept as a buffer, often leading to waste. Commonly employed by supply chain managers, ops teams, and cautious planners.

"We stocked just-in-case inventory until our warehouse looked like a museum of unsold dreams."

Related Terms: Lean methodology, Scope creep, Donkey work

K

IS FOR KPI BECAUSE KEEPING KEY PERFORMANCE INDICATORS KEENLY KNOWN KEEPS KINGDOMS FROM KAPUT.

KPI (KEY PERFORMANCE INDICATOR)

abbr. + n. A measurable value demonstrating how effectively objectives are achieved. Commonly employed by managers, analysts, and leadership to track performance.

"Our KPI said we hit our sales targets, ignoring that we bribed customers with free snacks and empty promises."

Related Terms: Conversion rate, ROI (Return on Investment), OKR

KYC (KNOW YOUR CUSTOMER)

abbr. + n. A process verifying clients' identities to prevent fraud and ensure compliance. Commonly employed by banks, financial institutions, and compliance teams.

"The KYC checks took so long I aged a year while waiting to prove I'm not a Nigerian prince."

Related Terms: AML (Anti-Money Laundering), Regulatory compliance, Due diligence

KEY TAKEAWAY

n. The main lesson or point to remember after a presentation, report, or discussion. Commonly employed by presenters, managers, and educators summarizing findings.

"The key takeaway from our monthly review? We're experts at making simple tasks complicated."

Related Terms: Learnings, Impact report, Case study

KEYBOARD WARRIOR

n. Someone who's aggressive or confrontational online but avoids face-to-face conflict. Commonly employed by coworkers, communities, and commentators mocking internet bravado.

"Our keyboard warrior attacked our design choices in the Slack channel but went silent when we offered a video call."

Related Terms: Knee-jerk reactions, Chime in, Bubble mentality

KNEE-JERK REACTIONS

n. Quick, reflexive decisions made without proper consideration. Commonly employed by managers, critics, and observers noting impulsive responses.

"Our knee-jerk reaction to declining sales was to double prices, which worked about as well as pouring gasoline on a fire."

Related Terms: Gut feel, HiPPO (Highest-Paid Person's Opinion), Scope creep

KOOL-AID DRINKER

(Noun) Someone who wholeheartedly believes in a company's vision, strategy, or leadership without question, often ignoring data or dissenting voices. Commonly employed by execs praising loyalty and cynics mocking blind faith.

"Our office Kool-Aid drinker applauded the CEO's every word, even the policy on 'mandatory high-fives.'"

Related Terms: My understanding, Stepford Worker, Drink the Kool-Aid

L

L IS FOR LEAN METHODOLOGY BECAUSE LIMITING LETHARGY AND LETTING LEAN LOGIC LEAD TO LESS LABOR AND LOFTIER LIBERATION.

LACK OF ACCOUNTABILITY

n. When individuals or teams fail to take responsibility for their actions. Commonly employed by managers, auditors, and critics of dysfunctional workplaces.

"There was a stunning lack of accountability, like a game of hot potato where everyone dropped the potato and blamed gravity."

Related Terms: CYA (Cover Your Ass), Fall guy, Above my paygrade

LACK OF VISION

n. The absence of clear, long-term direction or strategy. Commonly employed by employees, consultants, and analysts criticizing leadership.

"Our lack of vision meant we navigated strategy meetings like blindfolded tourists lost in a hedge maze."

Related Terms: Change management, Business transformation, Resistance to change

LANDLORD-TENANT LAW

n. Laws governing rights and responsibilities of landlords and tenants. Commonly employed by attorneys, property managers, and housing advocates.

"Our landlord-tenant law discussion ended with us realizing we had fewer rights than a library book overdue by a decade."

Related Terms: Lease agreement, Foreclosure, Escrow

LEAD GENERATION

n. Attracting potential customers (leads) who may be interested in a product or service. Commonly employed by marketers, sales teams, and growth hackers.

"Our lead generation strategy was so subtle, we might as well have screamed 'Buy now, you fools!' at passersby."

Related Terms: Conversion rate, A/B testing, Cross-channel marketing

LEADERSHIP PIPELINE

n. Identifying and developing future leaders within an organization. Commonly employed by HR, executives, and talent development programs.

"Our leadership pipeline looked more like a clogged pipe, producing managers who excelled at buzzwords, not results."

Related Terms: Aces in their places, Culture fit, Golden handcuffs

LEAN METHODOLOGY

n. An approach focusing on eliminating waste and improving value, often in product development. Commonly employed by operations, manufacturing, and agile teams.

"We applied lean methodology so thoroughly that we launched half-built features and called it 'market insight.'"

Related Terms: Lean startup, Lean waste, A/B testing

LEAN STARTUP

n. A methodology emphasizing rapid iteration, MVPs, and customer feedback in startups. Commonly employed by entrepreneurs, product managers, and early-stage companies.

"Our lean startup approach meant building a bare-bones app and hoping customers would love our skeleton of ambition."

Related Terms: MVP (Minimum Viable Product), A/B testing, Growth hacking

LEAN WASTE

n. Inefficiencies identified by Lean principles that don't add value. Commonly employed by process improvement teams, manufacturing lines, and quality managers.

"We identified lean waste when we noticed a team devoted solely to color-coding paper clips."

Related Terms: Lean methodology, Busy work, Donkey work

LEARNING

n. The process of gaining knowledge or skill through experience or training. Commonly employed by HR, L&D departments, and educators.

"Our approach to learning involved motivational posters and a mandatory webinar no one understood."

Related Terms: Learnings, Deep dive, Flesh out

LEARNINGS

n. Insights or lessons gained from an experience. Commonly employed by managers, teams, and facilitators after projects or retrospectives.

"The project failed spectacularly, but at least we got some learnings—like never trusting a plan scribbled on a napkin."

Related Terms: Key takeaway, Case study, Impact report

LEASE AGREEMENT

n. A contract between a landlord and tenant outlining rental terms. Commonly employed by property owners, tenants, and lawyers.

"Our lease agreement was so detailed it felt like we were signing away the rights to our future grandchildren."

Related Terms: Landlord-tenant law, Foreclosure, Real estate closing

LEASEHOLD ESTATE

n. The right to use and occupy property under a lease for a certain time. Commonly employed by tenants, landlords, and property managers in real estate.

"With our leasehold estate, we enjoyed temporary dominion over peeling wallpaper and suspicious odors."

Related Terms: Lease agreement, Investment property, Brownfield site

LET IT BAKE

phrase. Allowing an idea or decision to sit before taking action. Commonly employed by managers, creators, and strategists favoring reflection.

"We decided to let it bake, hoping the half-baked idea might magically rise into something edible."

Related Terms: Flesh out, Circle back, Deep dive

LET'S CIRCLE BACK ON THAT

phrase. Revisiting a topic later, often a polite way to defer discussion. Commonly employed by managers, presenters, and meeting facilitators.

"'Let's circle back on that' is code for 'I have no clue, let's hope we forget this ever came up.'"

Related Terms: Circle back, Brain dump, Consensus building

LEVER

n. An activity or project designed to generate actionable results. Commonly employed by strategists, executives, and operational managers.

"We tried to 'pull the lever' on cost-saving, but ended up with a lever that jammed and a budget that cried for mercy."

Related Terms: ROI (Return on Investment), Cost-benefit analysis, KPI (Key Performance Indicator)

LEVERAGE

v. To use resources, relationships, or tools effectively to achieve a goal. Commonly employed by managers, executives, and negotiators.

"We tried to leverage our marketing connections, which meant sending polite emails no one answered."

Related Terms: Lever, Buy-in, Conversion rate

LIBERALIZATION

n. Reducing government restrictions to encourage competition and market growth. Commonly employed by policymakers, economists, and trade analysts.

"After liberalization, the market was so free that anyone could fail with maximum efficiency."

Related Terms: Fiscal policy, Public policy, Economic stimulus

LISTING AGENT

n. A real estate agent representing the seller in a property transaction. Commonly employed by sellers and property owners looking to market their homes.

"Our listing agent praised every crack in the wall as 'rustic character,' proving optimism is a job requirement."

Related Terms: Buyer's agent, Investment property, Foreclosure

LOBBYING

n. Attempting to influence government decisions on behalf of an interest group or company. Commonly employed by corporations, advocacy groups, and lobbyists.

"Our lobbying efforts involved hiring someone who smiles while saying 'incentive alignment' and handing senators vague gift baskets."

Related Terms: Regulatory compliance, Government accountability, Public policy

LOCAL GOVERNMENT

n. City, town, or regional governance handling local services and policies. Commonly employed by citizens, policymakers, and community organizations.

"Our local government meeting ended with a heated debate on potholes, as if saving the world one crater at a time."

Related Terms: Public policy, Intergovernmental relations, Community outreach

LONG-TERM CARE

n. Services for individuals with chronic conditions or disabilities over extended periods. Commonly employed by healthcare providers, insurers, and assisted living facilities.

"Our strategy required long-term care—no, not just for customers, but for employees who endured year-long product rollouts."

Related Terms: Chronic care management, Care coordination, Value-based care

LOOKALIKE AUDIENCE

n. A marketing audience resembling an existing customer base in characteristics. Commonly employed by digital advertisers, marketers, and targeting specialists.

"We targeted a lookalike audience so precisely that even their goldfish had identical browsing habits."

Related Terms: Contextual targeting, Cross-channel marketing, A/B testing

LOOP IN

v. To include someone in a conversation or project, keeping them informed. Commonly employed by team leads, managers, and colleagues maintaining communication.

"They promised to loop me in, but I ended up in a loop of unanswered emails instead."

Related Terms: In the loop, Stakeholder engagement, Chime in

LOST IN THE WEEDS

phrase. Becoming overly focused on minor details, losing sight of the bigger picture. Commonly employed by managers, team leads, and mentors warning against nitpicking.

"Our manager got lost in the weeds discussing font choices while the entire product sank into irrelevance."

Related Terms: In the weeds, Heads down, Silo mentality

LOTS OF MOVING PARTS

phrase. A system or project with many interconnected, changing components. Commonly employed by project managers, execs, and team leads noting complexity.

"We had so many moving parts that our project resembled a Rube Goldberg machine powered by panic."

Related Terms: Break down silos, Process fatigue, Critical path

LOW-HANGING FRUIT

n. Easy targets or tasks likely to yield quick wins. Commonly employed by managers, strategists, and efficiency experts.

"We picked the low-hanging fruit first, then realized we were left with a tree full of wasp nests and regrets."

Related Terms: 80/20, A/B testing, Core competencies

M

IS FOR MINIMUM VIABLE PRODUCT (MVP) BECAUSE MAKING A MINIMALLY MAGICAL MODEL MINIMIZES MESS-UPS— MOVE FROM MAYBE TO MARKET!

MVP (MINIMUM VIABLE PRODUCT)

abbr. + n. The simplest version of a product with just enough features to satisfy early adopters. Commonly employed by startups, product managers, and lean teams.

"Our MVP was so minimal that calling it a 'product' was generous—it was more like a vague idea with a price tag."

Related Terms: Lean startup, A/B testing, Growth hacking

MACHINE LEARNING

n. A subset of AI where algorithms learn patterns from data and improve without explicit programming. Commonly employed by data scientists, engineers, and analysts in predictive modeling.

"Our machine learning model recommended selling umbrellas in the desert—clearly it was still 'learning.'"

Related Terms: Deep learning, Data management platform (DMP), Innovation

MACROMANAGER

n. A manager who attempts to control areas well outside their authority. Commonly employed by employees describing leaders who overreach into unrelated functions.

"Our macromanager supervised everything from corporate strategy down to which pen we used, resulting in universal annoyance."

Related Terms: Helicopter manager, Silo mentality, In the weeds

MAD MONEY

n. Funds or assets that can be spent impulsively or used unpredictably. Commonly employed by investors, CFOs, and individuals setting aside risk capital.

"We invested our mad money in a startup that sold artisanal light bulbs, so I guess 'mad' was the right word."

Related Terms: Dry powder, Risk management, Venture capital (VC)

MAGIC BULLET

n. A perfect solution that solves a complex problem easily. Commonly employed by managers, consultants, and teams hoping for quick fixes.

"We searched for a magic bullet to fix sales, but only found a rusty BB pellet of partial solutions."

Related Terms: Cost-benefit analysis, Deep dive, Disruption

MAINTENANCE BACKLOG

n. Accumulated maintenance issues that remain unresolved. Commonly employed by operations managers, facilities teams, and IT staff.

"Our maintenance backlog was so long it could star in its own horror film, 'The Return of the Broken Printer.'"

Related Terms: Broken workflow, Bottleneck, Lean waste

MAJOR PLAYER

n. An individual or company with significant influence or authority in a field. Commonly employed by analysts, media, and competitors identifying top market leaders.

"We wanted to be a major player, but we ended up as the benchwarmer no one remembers."

Related Terms: Game changer, Disruptive, Go to market

MAKE HAY

phrase. To take advantage of a favorable situation quickly. Commonly employed by managers, sales teams, and strategists urging seizing opportunities.

"We tried to make hay while the sun shone, but the sun was a flickering lightbulb in a dingy office."

Related Terms: Low-hanging fruit, A/B testing, Growth hacking

MAKE WAVES

phrase. To cause a stir or create noticeable change. Commonly employed by innovators, disruptors, and employees challenging the status quo.

"We made waves at the staff meeting by suggesting we do actual work instead of endless discussions—shocking stuff."

Related Terms: Disruption, Game changer, Go to market

MAKING SAUSAGE

phrase. Referring to messy behind-the-scenes processes that are unappealing. Commonly employed by insiders acknowledging the complexity of production or decision-making.

"Our project planning was like making sausage—lots of grinding and mystery ingredients, and no one wants to know the details."

Related Terms: Process fatigue, Broken workflow, Flogging a dead horse

MALICIOUS OBEDIENCE

n. Following orders exactly to highlight flaws or create problems intentionally. Commonly employed by employees and subordinates irritated by rigid commands.

"When told to send every email in caps, our malicious obedience ensured customers got SHOUTY NEWSLETTERS until the boss begged for mercy."

Related Terms: Micromanagement, Helicopter manager, CYA (Cover Your Ass)

MANAGEMENT BY WALKING AROUND

n. A leadership style where managers frequently roam the workplace to observe and engage with employees. Commonly employed by hands-on leaders, supervisors, and certain management philosophies.

"Management by walking around turned into 'Management by lurking awkwardly' in the break room."

Related Terms: Engage, Facipulate, Consensus building

MANAGEMENT PORN

n. Overly long, unnecessary slide decks or documents stuffed with buzzwords. Commonly employed by employees mocking excessive corporate presentations.

"The CEO's presentation was management porn—100 slides of synergy and no climax of understanding."

Related Terms: Management speak, Bullshit bingo, Fluff

MANAGEMENT SPEAK

n. Overuse of corporate jargon or buzzwords lacking substance. Commonly employed by employees, critics, and outsiders mocking office language.

"After an hour of management speak, we concluded that 'leveraging synergies' meant nothing more than 'keep doing what you do.'"

Related Terms: Bullshit bingo, Corporate lingo, Fluff

MANDATE

n. An official order or requirement. Commonly employed by executives, policy-makers, and project leads directing actions.

"They gave us a mandate to improve results, but provided no resources, making it less a strategy and more a dare."

Related Terms: Executive decision, Regulatory compliance, Above my paygrade

MANEL

n. A panel composed entirely of men, often criticized for lack of diversity. Commonly employed by diversity advocates, conference organizers, and critics calling for inclusion.

"Our conference featured a manel on women's leadership, illustrating irony so thick you could carve it."

Related Terms: Glass ceiling, Elitism, Culture fit

MARINATE

v. Taking time to think about an idea privately before responding or deciding. Commonly employed by managers, colleagues, and decision-makers preferring reflection.

"We decided to let the proposal marinate—because nothing says progress like leaving it to sit until stale."

Related Terms: Let it bake, Circle back, Flesh out

MARKET ANALYSIS

n. Evaluating supply, demand, and conditions in a particular market. Commonly employed by strategists, marketers, and product managers to inform decisions.

"Our market analysis revealed customers want cheaper products that actually work, a radical concept indeed."

Related Terms: Go-to-market strategy, Conversion rate, Customer journey

MARKET-FACING

adj. Roles or activities interacting directly with customers. Commonly employed by sales teams, marketing, and customer support functions.

"Our market-facing team smiled through clenched teeth as they explained yet again why the product was delayed."

Related Terms: Customer-centric, Client-centric, Cross-channel marketing

MARKETECTURE

n. Marketing materials focusing heavily on technical specs or diagrams. Commonly employed by product marketers and sales engineers impressing prospects with complexity.

"Our brochure was pure marketecture: pretty diagrams, zero explanation—just how the engineers like it."

Related Terms: Fluff, Management speak, Bullshit bingo

MATRICES

n. Diagrams or frameworks used to classify information or justify decisions. Commonly employed by consultants, strategists, and decision-makers organizing data.

"We built so many matrices that our decisions looked like a crossword puzzle of confusion."

Related Terms: Framework, Granular, Flesh out

MATRIX TEAM

n. A team composed of members from various departments working together. Commonly employed by complex projects, cross-functional initiatives, and large organizations.

"Our matrix team combined experts from marketing, finance, and IT, ensuring no one understood each other's acronyms."

Related Terms: Break down silos, Consensus building, Silo mentality

MCJOB

n. A job perceived as low-status, low-pay, and offering few opportunities for growth. Commonly employed by critics of certain service roles or dead-end positions.

"They called it a McJob, but at least flipping burgers comes with clear instructions—unlike our latest project."

Related Terms: Donkey work, Busy work, Hostage mentality

MEANDERTHAL

n. An individual who struggles to articulate thoughts effectively, wandering aimlessly in explanations. Commonly employed humorously by colleagues describing confusing communicators.

"Our project update turned into a meanderthal's paradise, with sentences wandering off cliffs of nonsense."

Related Terms: Management speak, Fluff, In the weeds

MEAT AND POTATOES

n. The foundational or essential components of something. Commonly employed by managers, writers, and leaders focusing on core elements.

"We finally got to the meat and potatoes of the proposal after 30 slides of seasoning and garnish no one asked for."

Related Terms: Core competencies, Key takeaway, Meat on the bone

MEAT ON THE BONE

n. Profits or value left in an opportunity, indicating potential gain. Commonly employed by investors, analysts, and managers seeking untapped resources.

"Our revenue projections had lots of meat on the bone, if you enjoy chewy, flavorless gristle."

Related Terms: Low-hanging fruit, Gain traction, Cost-benefit analysis

MEDICAL BILLING

n. The process of submitting and following up on claims with health insurers for payment. Commonly employed by healthcare providers, billing specialists, and insurance companies.

"Medical billing turned a routine check-up into an epic quest for payment codes and lost invoices."

Related Terms: ICD-10 codes, Fee-for-service, Care coordination

MEDICAL HOME

n. A healthcare model with a primary provider coordinating all aspects of a patient's care. Commonly employed by healthcare reformers, clinics, and integrated systems.

"Our medical home promised coordinated care, but we got a chaotic game of telephone between specialists instead."

Related Terms: Integrated care, ACO (Accountable care organization), Chronic care management

MEDICAL MALPRACTICE

n. Professional negligence by a healthcare provider causing harm to a patient. Commonly employed by lawyers, insurers, and patient advocates.

"After the malpractice suit, the hospital tried rebranding by hanging motivational posters in the hallway—problem solved?"

Related Terms: Regulatory compliance, Care coordination, Due diligence

MEDICAL NECESSITY

n. Healthcare services deemed essential for treating a condition. Commonly employed by insurers, doctors, and regulatory bodies deciding coverage.

"Our insurer questioned the 'medical necessity' of not dying from a treatable illness—thanks for the expert input."

Related Terms: Value-based care, Capitation, Fee-for-service

MEDICALLY NECESSARY

adj. Required treatments or services judged essential for proper patient care. Commonly employed by healthcare providers, insurers, and care coordinators.

"We debated if the procedure was medically necessary, as if patients enjoy costly surgeries for fun."

Related Terms: Medical necessity, Care coordination, Value-based care

MEDICARE ADVANTAGE

n. A type of Medicare plan offered by private insurers as an alternative to traditional Medicare. Commonly employed by seniors, insurers, and policymakers examining healthcare options.

"Medicare Advantage gave us more 'choices,' all equally perplexing and expensive—how delightful."

Related Terms: HMO (Health Maintenance Organization), Capitation, Value-based care

MEDICARE PART D

n. A federal program helping Medicare recipients pay for prescription drugs. Commonly employed by seniors, pharmacists, and insurers managing prescription coverage.

"Medicare Part D taught us that even saving on prescriptions involves navigating a labyrinth of acronyms."

Related Terms: Medical billing, Value-based care, Chronic care management

MEDICATION THERAPY MANAGEMENT (MTM)

n. Services by pharmacists to optimize medication use and improve patient outcomes. Commonly employed by pharmacies, Medicare plans, and healthcare systems.

"MTM sounded progressive until we realized it just meant a lecture on not mixing cough syrup and tequila."

Related Terms: Chronic care management, Care coordination, Value-based care

MEDIOCRE LEADERSHIP

n. Leaders who lack vision, strategic thinking, or the ability to inspire teams. Commonly employed by employees, consultants, and critics describing bland management.

"Our mediocre leadership team held a strategy session that ended with a to-do list of 'Try harder, I guess.'"

Related Terms: Lack of vision, Empty suit, Resistance to change

MEDIOCRITY

n. Being average or subpar, lacking ambition or innovation. Commonly employed by employees, critics, and observers bemoaning lackluster efforts.

"We embraced mediocrity, slapping 'Good enough!' stickers on failed prototypes and calling it a day."

Related Terms: Mediocre leadership, Bubble mentality, Culture fit

MEETING ASSASSIN

n. A person who dominates or derails meetings with excessive commentary or negativity. Commonly employed by attendees mocking disruptive colleagues.

"The meeting assassin struck again, turning a five-minute check-in into a TED Talk on office temperature preferences."

Related Terms: Bullshit bingo, Malicious obedience, Management speak

MEETING FILL

n. Employees who attend meetings but contribute little or no value, just filling seats. Commonly employed by observers noting token attendance.

"We added meeting fill to impress the boss with a big turnout, even if half the attendees contributed blank stares."

Related Terms: Just filling seats, Busy work, Dead weight

MEETING HELL

n. Excessive, inefficient, or unproductive meetings draining time and resources. Commonly employed by employees, managers, and consultants lamenting pointless gatherings.

"Our calendar descended into meeting hell, a bottomless pit where agendas go to die and coffee mugs cry for mercy."

Related Terms: Groundhog Day, Bullshit bingo, In the weeds

MELT-DOWN

n. A total failure or collapse of a product, service, or system. Commonly employed by employees, media, and stakeholders describing catastrophic events.

"After the system meltdown, we blamed Mercury in retrograde since logical explanations had fled the building."

Related Terms: Dumpster fire, Death spiral, Crisis mode

MENTAL HEALTH PARITY

n. Equal coverage of mental health and substance use treatment as physical healthcare. Commonly employed by insurers, lawmakers, and advocates for equality in care.

"Our insurance boasted mental health parity, but navigating the claim forms required therapy on its own."

Related Terms: Value-based care, Care coordination, HMO (Health Maintenance Organization)

MERITOCRACY

n. A system where advancement is based on individual achievement rather than arbitrary factors. Commonly employed by HR, executives, and policymakers praising fairness (or pretending to).

"We claimed to be a meritocracy, yet promotions were based on who complimented the boss's tie selection."

Related Terms: Aces in their places, Core competencies, Glass ceiling

META IGNORANCE

n. Unawareness of one's own knowledge gaps. Commonly employed by critics, analysts, and educators noting profound cluelessness.

"Our exec's meta ignorance was so profound he presented 'Unknown Unknowns' as a growth strategy."

Related Terms: Acluistic, Mushroom principle, Bubble mentality

MIC DROP

n. A bold or decisive statement ending a discussion dramatically. Commonly employed by presenters, speakers, and employees delivering final zingers.

"After announcing layoffs during a 'holiday cheer' meeting, the CFO's speech felt like a mic drop from the Grinch."

Related Terms: Elevator pitch, Key takeaway, Chime in

MICKEY MOUSE

adj. Describing a simplistic solution failing to address complex issues. Commonly employed by employees, critics, and commentators mocking superficial fixes.

"Our Mickey Mouse fix was slapping duct tape on a server meltdown and calling it 'proactive maintenance.'"

Related Terms: Cookie-cutter approach, Fluff, MVP (Minimum Viable Product)

MICROMANAGEMENT

n. Excessive control over employees' work, undermining autonomy and trust. Commonly employed by employees and advisors warning against controlling leadership styles.

"Under micromanagement, even choosing a stapler color required a committee and a SWOT analysis."

Related Terms: Helicopter manager, Malicious obedience, In the weeds

MILK

v. To exploit a situation or resource for maximum benefit. Commonly employed by insiders, employees, and critics noting opportunistic behavior.

"We tried to milk our one success story so hard it soured into cringe-worthy bragging."

Related Terms: Bottom feeder, Cutthroat, Chainsaw consultant

MINDSHARE

n. The level of public awareness or attention a brand or concept receives. Commonly employed by marketers, brand managers, and advertisers.

"We aimed for mindshare but got a fleeting mental hiccup—customers forgot us faster than a bad joke."

Related Terms: Cross-channel marketing, Influencer marketing, A/B testing

MISALIGNMENT OF OBJECTIVES

(Noun) When different teams or departments have conflicting goals, causing confusion, inefficiency, and failure to meet overall targets. Commonly employed by managers, project leads, and analysts noting a company heading in different directions internally.

"Our misalignment of objectives ensured our left hand never knew what our right hand was doing."

Related Terms: Silo mentality, Above my paygrade, Resistance to change

MISMATCH BETWEEN DEMAND AND SUPPLY

(Noun) When production doesn't align with market needs, resulting in either lost sales opportunities or excess inventory waste. Commonly employed by operations, supply chain managers, and forecasters who can't quite hit the sweet spot.

"Our mismatch between demand and supply meant we had warehouses full of products nobody wanted."

Related Terms: Overproduction, Low-hanging fruit, Burn rate

MISSION CRITICAL

(Adj.) Highlighting tasks or goals considered essential and urgent, often invoked to stress immediate attention. Commonly employed by leaders, project leads, and decision-makers wanting everyone to drop everything else.

"Completing these reports was mission critical, so naturally we started at 4:59 PM."

Related Terms: ASAP, Above-board, Critical path

MISSION STATEMENT

(Noun) A formal summary of a nonprofit's aims and values, guiding its decisions and strategies. Commonly employed by nonprofit boards, donors, and staff who appreciate a tidy summary of purpose.

"Our mission statement read like poetry, but delivered results like stale toast."

Related Terms: Core values, Nonprofit sector, Transparency

MISSION-DRIVEN

(Adj.) Describing a nonprofit focused on achieving a specific social or charitable goal rather than profit. Commonly employed by founders, donors, and staff who believe impact beats revenue margins.

"Our mission-driven group insisted that results mattered more than marketing slogans."

Related Terms: Nonprofit partnership, Capacity building, Value proposition

MOM-AND-POP

(Adj.) Referring to a small, often family-owned business with limited scale and local reach. Commonly employed by community leaders, local customers, and investors who love authenticity.

"Our mom-and-pop shop sold handmade goods the big chains wouldn't bother with."

Related Terms: Mommy track, Culture fit, BAU (Business as usual)

MOMMY TRACK

(Noun) A career path seen as offering limited growth, often associated with balancing family duties. Commonly employed by HR, career coaches, and cynics pointing out hidden biases in promotion plans.

"Stuck on the mommy track, she watched others climb ladders she was never offered."

Related Terms: Glass ceiling, No room to grow, Job security theatre

MONDAY MORNING QUARTERBACK

(Noun) A person who critiques decisions only after outcomes are known, without contributing initially. Commonly employed by coworkers and commentators who delight in hindsight superiority.

"Our Monday morning quarterback explained exactly how we should have won after we lost."

Related Terms: Bite the bullet, Blame game, Herding cats

MOONSHOT DIVISION

(Noun) An internal group exploring wildly ambitious, long-term projects with high risk and high potential reward. Commonly employed by innovative companies, R&D labs, and dreamers who think small steps are boring.

"Our Moonshot Division pitched teleportation booths while we struggled to fix the coffee machine."

Related Terms: Skunkworks, Disruption, Innovation

MOUSE POTATO

(Noun) A person spending excessive hours online or at a computer, mirroring the "couch potato" concept. Commonly employed by HR, IT support, and concerned colleagues who see no daylight in your schedule.

"Our mouse potato intern clicked through spreadsheets like a zombie scrolling an endless feed."

Related Terms: Clock watcher, Heads down, Workstream

MOUTH-BREATHER

(Noun) A derogatory term implying someone lacks intelligence or sophistication. Commonly employed by rude coworkers, frustrated team leads, and snarky Slack channels.

"After his tenth lame excuse, the VP muttered 'mouth-breather' under her breath."

Related Terms: Negatron, Dead weight, Multi-slacker

MOVE THE GOAL POSTS

(Phrase) Changing objectives mid-project, often making success harder to achieve. Commonly employed by managers shifting blame, execs raising standards, and teams groaning in protest.

"Just when we hit the target, they moved the goal posts, demanding even more revisions."

Related Terms: Scope creep, Bottleneck, Circle back

MOVE THE NEEDLE

(Phrase) Achieving meaningful, noticeable progress. Commonly employed by leaders, strategists, and sales teams aiming for tangible improvement.

"We finally moved the needle after ditching half our useless meetings."

Related Terms: Quick win, High level, Deep dive

MOVE THINGS FORWARD

(Phrase) To advance a project or task toward completion. Commonly employed by managers, PMs, and colleagues tired of endless status updates.

"Let's move things forward so we can stop discussing this for eternity."

Related Terms: Nail jelly to the wall, Make hay, In the pipeline

MOVING THE GOALPOSTS

(Phrase) Another phrase for changing established criteria mid-project, frustrating everyone involved. Commonly employed by top brass wriggling out of promised outcomes.

"They're moving the goalposts again—apparently perfection wasn't enough."

Related Terms: Move the goal posts, Marinate, Milestone

MUCUS TROOPER

(Noun) The perennial sick colleague who never shakes the worst cold. Commonly employed by teams hoping they'd just take a sick day.

"Our mucus trooper sniffled through the pitch, adding ambiance no one requested."

Related Terms: Mushroom principle, Herding turtles, Stress puppy

MULTI-SLACKER

(Noun) Someone skilled at being unproductive across multiple tasks at once. Commonly employed by frustrated managers and coworkers who wonder how this is a talent.

"Our multi-slacker failed at three projects simultaneously—impressive in a twisted way."

Related Terms: Dead weight, Donkey work, Time-poor

MULTI-USE DEVELOPMENT

(Noun) A project combining residential, commercial, and other spaces in one location. Commonly employed by urban planners, developers, and investors hoping for synergy.

"Our multi-use development included apartments, shops, and a random alpaca petting zone."

Related Terms: Greenfield site, Brownfield site, Build-to-suit

MULTIFAMILY UNIT

(Noun) A building with multiple separate living units for different households. Commonly employed by real estate agents, landlords, and tenants who enjoy shared walls.

"Our multifamily unit housed feuding neighbors who turned the hall into a gossip exchange."

Related Terms: Occupancy rate, NOI, Cap rate

MUPPET SHUFFLE

(Noun) Moving problematic employees around instead of addressing underlying issues. Commonly employed by HR avoiding tough decisions, hoping reshuffles hide the mess.

"After the muppet shuffle, we ended up with the same problems in new cubicles."

Related Terms: Dead weight, Silo mentality, Chainsaw consultant

MUSHROOM PRINCIPLE

(Noun) A management style keeping employees in the dark and feeding them nonsense. Commonly employed by bosses who fear transparency and love surprise panic.

"Under the mushroom principle, we learned about deadlines from the janitor's hints."

Related Terms: Transparency, Silo mentality

MY UNDERSTANDING

(Phrase) Expressing an interpretation or opinion without certainty. Commonly employed by employees hedging statements to avoid blame.

"My understanding is we're fine—unless we're completely doomed, of course."

Related Terms: Above my paygrade, Context, Flesh out

N

N IS FOR NONPROFIT SECTOR BECAUSE NAVIGATING NONPROFIT NUANCES NURTURES NOBLE NOTIONS—NO NEED FOR NARCISSISTIC NET GAINS!

NAIL JELLY TO THE WALL

phrase. Attempting something incredibly difficult or nearly impossible. Commonly employed by project leads and strategists describing hopeless tasks.

"Finishing that report in an hour is like trying to nail jelly to the wall."

Related Terms: Boil the ocean, Herding cats, Pushing wet spaghetti

NATIVE ADVERTISING

n. Ads blending seamlessly into platform content. Commonly employed by marketers who hope audiences won't notice the sales pitch.

"Our native advertising was so subtle that readers thought we were poet laureates of vacuums."

Related Terms: Contextual targeting, Ad creatives, Sympvertizing

NATIVE CONTENT

n. Content resembling a platform's regular posts, making ads seem natural. Commonly employed by content creators and influencers hiding promotions in plain sight.

"Our native content matched the platform so well users asked if our ad was user-generated."

Related Terms: Native advertising, Cookie-cutter approach, Branding

NEGATRON

n. A person fixated on negatives, draining optimism at every turn. Commonly employed by coworkers referencing the office gloom-bringer.

"Ted, the negatron, insisted free donuts heralded obesity, not celebration."

Related Terms: Bubble mentality, Mushroom principle, Cutting corners

NET NEUTRALITY

n. The principle that all internet data should be treated equally. Commonly employed by policymakers, activists, and consumers demanding fairness.

"Mentioning net neutrality made Gary's eyes glaze—he just wanted faster cat videos."

Related Terms: Regulatory compliance, Open banking, Carbon pricing

NET OPERATING INCOME (NOI)

n. Income from property minus operating expenses, excluding mortgage. Commonly employed by real estate investors doing fancy math.

"Our NOI looked great until we realized no one actually paid rent."

Related Terms: Cap rate, Burn rate, Greenfield site

NET-NET

n. A distilled summary of main points after all details considered. Commonly employed by execs and consultants needing a bottom line.

"After hours of chatter, the net-net was 'Sell something, maybe.'"

Related Terms: Key takeaway, Executive summary, High level

NETWORKING EFFECTS

n. Value increases as more people use the product. Commonly employed by startups and tech firms preaching viral destiny.

"Our app's networking effects made even haters invite friends—misery loves company."

Related Terms: Network-centric, Viral marketing, Scale up

NEW GUY GENE

n. The friendly, eager demeanor of newcomers before cynicism sets in. Commonly employed by HR and vets observing fresh recruits still smiling.

"Dave's new guy gene shone as he volunteered to make coffee for everyone."

Related Terms: Culture fit, Mom-and-pop, Clock watcher

NEWS SANDWICH

n. A lunch break spent catching up on current events. Commonly employed by knowledge workers multitasking midday.

"My news sandwich break ended with me choking on election updates—delicious."

Related Terms: Brownfield site, Community outreach, Public opinion polling

NO ROOM TO GROW

phrase. Limited opportunities for advancement or development. Commonly employed by frustrated staff blocked from promotions.

"Staring at the org chart, Pat realized no room to grow meant staying stuck forever."

Related Terms: Glass ceiling, Dead weight, Donkey work

NO WORRIES

phrase. Informal reassurance that no problem exists. Commonly employed by colleagues and managers downplaying issues.

"'No worries,' said the boss as profits sank—apparently panic's optional."

Related Terms: It is what it is, Above-board, Over-engineering

NONPROFIT BRANDING

n. Managing a nonprofit's public image, logo, and messaging. Commonly employed by PR teams and development officers feigning purity.

"Our nonprofit branding screamed 'We care!' while we debated tote bag colors."

Related Terms: Corporate sponsorship, Core values, Transparent fundraising

NONPROFIT COMPLIANCE

n. Adherence to nonprofit laws and regulations. Commonly employed by boards and auditors ensuring do-gooding isn't done badly.

"Our nonprofit compliance binder weighed more than our mission statement."

Related Terms: Nonprofit governance, Due diligence, 501(c)(3)

NONPROFIT GOVERNANCE

n. Systems directing and controlling a nonprofit, often a board of directors. Commonly employed by trustees ensuring no one steals the donation jar.

"Nonprofit governance sparked more debates about pen budgets than feeding the needy."

Related Terms: Nonprofit sector, Endowment fund, Business transformation

NONPROFIT PARTNERSHIP

n. Collaborations between nonprofits or nonprofits and businesses for shared goals. Commonly employed by grantmakers and community leaders trying synergy without profits.

"After forming a nonprofit partnership, we discovered we shared donors and their polite yawns."

Related Terms: <u>Consensus building</u>, <u>Corporate lingo</u>, <u>Community outreach</u>

NONPROFIT SECTOR

n. The economy's part with charities and NGOs, no profits needed. Commonly employed by volunteers and donors hoping goodwill trumps greed.

"In the nonprofit sector, social impact often meant old T-shirts as moral trophies."

Related Terms: <u>Nonprofit governance</u>, <u>Nonprofit compliance</u>, <u>Charitable giving</u>

NURSE PRACTITIONER (NP)

n. A trained nurse who can diagnose and treat conditions, often a primary care hero. Commonly employed by healthcare systems short on doctors.

"Our NP answered more questions in an hour than management does all fiscal year."

Related Terms: <u>Accountable care organization (ACO)</u>, <u>Value-based care</u>, <u>Capitation</u>

O

IS FOR ONBOARDING BECAUSE ORGANIZING OPTIMAL ONBOARDING OFFSETS ONGOING OBSTACLES, OFFICIALLY!

OOO (OUT OF OFFICE)

(Abbreviation) Indicating absence or unavailability. Commonly employed by anyone escaping the email avalanche.

"My OOO said 'Gone Fishing'—colleagues knew I meant fishing for fewer meetings."

Related Terms: <u>DNB</u>, <u>EOD</u>, <u>Face time</u>

OCCUPANCY RATE

n. Percentage of rental units occupied. Commonly employed by property managers counting pennies.

"Our occupancy rate soared, but tenants were all cousins crashing rent-free."

Related Terms: <u>NOI</u>, <u>Cap rate</u>, <u>Maintenance backlog</u>

OFF THE RECORD

(Phrase) Private conversation not for public mention. Commonly employed by insiders with juicy secrets.

"'Off the record,' whispered the CFO, before spilling truths that could topple empires."

Related Terms: <u>Chatham House Rules</u>, <u>Under the radar</u>, <u>Mushroom principle</u>

OFFLINE

(Adj.) Not connected or unavailable. Commonly employed by IT staff and remote workers ignoring Slack.

"I went offline and returned to 60 unread emails—digital horror indeed."

Related Terms: <u>OOO</u>, <u>EOD</u>, <u>DNB</u>

OMBUDSMAN

(Noun) Official investigating complaints for fairness. Commonly employed by public agencies and unions craving justice.

"When the ombudsman arrived, our blame game turned into nervous silence."

Related Terms: Whistleblower, Regulatory compliance, Interagency cooperation

ON BOARD

(Phrase) Agreeing or supporting an idea. Commonly employed by managers praying for nodding heads.

"Half the team was on board, the other half mentally jumped ship."

Related Terms: Buy-in, Consensus building, Aha moment

ON MY RADAR

(Phrase) Acknowledging something as noteworthy. Commonly employed by execs juggling endless alerts.

"'It's on my radar,' said Lee, whose radar was a cluttered junkyard of tasks."

Related Terms: In the loop, Key takeaway, Visibility to

ON THE SAME PAGE

(Phrase) Sharing understanding or agreement. Commonly employed by teams aiming for unity.

"We got on the same page, though that page was blank—fitting."

Related Terms: Consensus building, Marinate, Alignment

ONBOARDING

(Noun) Integrating newcomers into a system. Commonly employed by HR and trainers.

"Our onboarding included a 300-slide deck and a stiff handshake—thrilling."

Related Terms: Incubator, Accelerator, New guy gene

OPEN BANKING

(Noun) Allowing third-party services around bank data. Commonly employed by fintech dreamers.

"Open banking: we gave outsiders our data and prayed for miracles."

Related Terms: DeFi, Blockchain, Regulatory compliance

OPEN THE FLOODGATES

(Phrase) Initiate actions causing overwhelming response. Commonly employed by marketers fearing mob scenes.

"Announcing free snacks opened the floodgates to stampeding interns."

Related Terms: Over-engineering, Low-hanging fruit, Nail jelly to the wall

OPTICS

(Noun) The perception or impression of a situation. Commonly employed by PR smoothing surfaces.

"The optics of our 'innovation lab' were great—just a broom closet with LED strips."

Related Terms: Transparency, Above-board, Bullshit bingo

OPTIMIZE

(Verb) Improve performance or outcomes. Commonly employed by consultants tweaking everything.

"We optimized excuses, not results—progress?"

Related Terms: Lean methodology, A/B testing, Delta

OPTIMIZE

v. To make something as effective or functional as possible. Commonly employed by analysts, engineers, and strategists improving efficiency.

"We tried to optimize our workflow by adding more steps and approvals—mission accomplished if chaos was our goal."

Related Terms: A/B testing, Lean methodology, Cost-benefit analysis

OPTIONALITY

n. Maintaining various choices or alternatives for future flexibility. Commonly employed by strategists, investors, and product teams hedging bets.

"We hoarded optionality like doomsday preppers, ending up paralyzed by too many maybes."

Related Terms: Buy-in, Gain traction, Lean startup

OUT OF POCKET

phrase. Being unavailable or unreachable, or paying expenses personally. Commonly employed by employees, managers, and colleagues indicating absence or personal expense.

"I'm out of pocket this afternoon, which is corporate code for 'I'm hiding from Slack notifications.'"

Related Terms: DNB (Do Not Bother/Book), FYI (For Your Information), EOD (End Of Day)

OUT-OF-POCKET MAXIMUM

n. The most a patient pays for healthcare in a plan year before the insurer covers 100%. Commonly employed by insurers, patients, and benefits coordinators.

"Our out-of-pocket maximum felt like a polite way of saying, 'Empty your wallet, then we'll consider helping.'"

Related Terms: HSA (Health Savings Account), Capitation, Value-based care

OUTDATED TECHNOLOGY

n. Using old or obsolete systems leading to inefficiency and higher costs. Commonly employed by IT, operations, and consultants urging modernization.

"We ran on outdated technology so ancient, I expected to find hieroglyphics in the user manual."

Related Terms: Digital transformation, Broken workflow, Lean methodology

OUTPATIENT CARE

n. Medical services not requiring an overnight hospital stay. Commonly employed by clinics, hospitals, and insurers focusing on cost-effective treatment.

"Our outpatient care solution sped patients in and out so fast they barely had time to find the exit."

Related Terms: Inpatient care, Care coordination, Value-based care

OUTSOURCING

v. Contracting external parties to perform tasks normally done in-house. Commonly employed by companies seeking cost savings, expertise, or flexibility.

"We outsourced so much that someday even our company name might be handled by a third-party vendor."

Related Terms: Lean methodology, Cost-benefit analysis, Buy-in

OVER THE WALL

phrase. Passing responsibilities or information to another group without proper follow-up. Commonly employed by coworkers, managers, and project leads criticizing siloed handoffs.

"We threw the data over the wall to IT, then acted shocked when they had no clue what to do with it."

Related Terms: Break down silos, Silo mentality, Circle back

OVER-ENGINEERING

v. Adding unnecessary complexity or features leading to wasted resources. Commonly employed by engineers, designers, and PMs warning against feature bloat.

"Our over-engineered solution had more buttons than a spaceship, all just to open a spreadsheet."

Related Terms: Lean methodology, MVP (Minimum Viable Product), Cookie-cutter approach

OVERPRODUCTION

n. Producing more than needed, causing waste. Commonly employed by operations, Lean practitioners, and supply chain managers.

"We rejoiced at overproduction, because who doesn't love warehouses full of unsellable inventory?"

Related Terms: Lean methodology, Lean waste, Just-in-case inventory

OVERPROMISE, UNDERDELIVER

phrase. Making commitments not met, leading to disappointment. Commonly employed by customers, critics, and managers calling out failed expectations.

"We promised a groundbreaking app but delivered a glitchy slideshow—classic overpromise, underdeliver style."

Related Terms: Broken record, Low-hanging fruit, Cost-benefit analysis

P
IS FOR PHILANTHROPY BECAUSE PLACING PENNIES TOWARDS POSITIVE PURPOSES PROFOUNDLY PAYS IN PUBLIC PERCEPTION.

PAC (PERFECTLY ABSOLUTELY CLEAR)

abbr. + phrase. Expressing total certainty or clarity. Commonly employed jokingly by teams, managers, and writers confirming understanding.

"'PAC' means we're absolutely sure—until we find out we were absolutely wrong five minutes later."

Related Terms: Key takeaway, Executive summary, POV (Point Of View)

POC (POINT OF CONTACT)

abbr. + n. The primary person for communication or coordination in a project or relationship. Commonly employed by PMs, HR, and stakeholders centralizing communication.

"Our POC vanished into a black hole of emails, leaving us guessing who's actually in charge."

Related Terms: Stakeholder engagement, In the loop, Loop in

POV (POINT OF VIEW)

abbr. + n. An individual's perspective or opinion on an issue. Commonly employed by analysts, presenters, and team members clarifying stances.

"From my POV, our strategy is like a blindfolded dart throw—aimless and slightly dangerous."

Related Terms: Key takeaway, Counterfactual, Gut feel

PPO (PREFERRED PROVIDER ORGANIZATION)

abbr. + n. A health insurance plan offering more provider choice, often at higher costs. Commonly employed by patients, HR, and insurers balancing flexibility and expense.

"Our PPO let us pick any doctor, which was great until we saw the bill and fainted in the waiting room."

Related Terms: HMO (Health Maintenance Organization), Value-based care, Capitation

PACESETTER

n. An entity setting standards or trends in a market or field. Commonly employed by analysts, media, and industry observers noting leaders.

"We aimed to be a pacesetter but ended up pacing nervously in the hallway without setting much of anything."

Related Terms: Major player, Game changer, Disruptive

PADDLE ON BOTH SIDES

phrase. Exerting maximum effort to achieve a goal. Commonly employed humorously by managers or teammates encouraging full commitment.

"We paddled on both sides, churning water like eager beavers, yet still drifted in circles."

Related Terms: Giving 110%, Go to market, Hit the ground running

PAIN POINT

n. A specific problem or challenge faced by customers or teams. Commonly employed by product managers, marketers, and sales identifying opportunities.

"The login process was such a pain point that customers considered carrier pigeons more reliable."

Related Terms: Customer journey, Conversion rate, Chronic care management

PANAM

v. (Slang for 'take over abruptly' - not fully defined originally) Commonly employed jokingly or by insiders describing a sudden takeover.

"The new manager tried to PanAm our project, swooping in like a hungry hawk on a mouse with low self-esteem."

Related Terms: Playing politics, Helicopter manager, Macromanager

PANACEA

n. A universal solution intended to resolve all problems. Commonly employed by strategists, critics, and commentators noting overhyped cures.

"We pitched our software as a panacea, ignoring that customers wanted cures, not mythical potions."

Related Terms: Magic bullet, Disruption, Cost-benefit analysis

PANIC-DRIVEN DECISIONS

n. Choices made hastily under pressure, often resulting in poor outcomes. Commonly employed by employees, managers, and critics noting reactive strategies.

"Our panic-driven decision to slash prices made customers suspicious and accountants weep."

Related Terms: Knee-jerk reactions, Crisis mode, Overpromise, underdeliver

PAPER

v. To formally document or record an agreement, action, or transaction. Commonly employed by legal teams, admin staff, and negotiators.

"They asked us to paper the deal, which meant producing enough documents to kill a small forest."

Related Terms: Hard copy, Due diligence, Regulatory compliance

PAPER CUT

n. A minor but irritating problem or issue. Commonly employed by employees and managers acknowledging small annoyances.

"Our latest glitch was a paper cut of a bug—annoying and pointless, causing more grumbles than real harm."

Related Terms: Flogging a dead horse, Donkey work, Busy work

PAPER SHREDDER

n. A device or process for destroying documents. Commonly employed by offices, archives, and compliance teams for confidentiality.

"We fed the failed strategy into the paper shredder, a fitting end for a proposal that made no sense."

Related Terms: Paper shreddering, CYA (Cover Your Ass), Hard copy

PAPER SHREDDING

n. Discarding or disregarding work, often due to changing priorities or poor planning. Commonly employed by project leads, managers, or teams forced to abandon efforts.

"After months of effort, management started paper shredding our project plans like confetti at a disappointment parade."

Related Terms: Dumpster fire, Flogging a dead horse, Scope creep

PARADIGM SHIFT

n. A fundamental change in approach or underlying assumptions. Commonly employed by execs, thought leaders, and strategists highlighting big changes.

"Our 'paradigm shift' was just rebranding old ideas as new, hoping nobody noticed the same stale logic."

Related Terms: Disruption, Business transformation, Innovation

PARKING LOT

(Noun) A metaphorical holding area for ideas, questions, or topics set aside during a meeting for later discussion, assuming "later" ever arrives. Commonly employed by facilitators, managers, and anyone dodging off-topic rants.

"We tossed half the agenda into the parking lot, where items go to quietly fade from memory."

Related Terms: Circle back, Marinate, Off the record

PATIENT PORTAL

n. An online tool allowing patients to access health records and communicate with providers. Commonly employed by healthcare providers, patients, and IT in medical settings.

"The patient portal let me view my test results faster, so I could panic in real-time rather than waiting by the mailbox."

Related Terms: EHR (Electronic Health Record), Care coordination, Chronic care management

PATIENT SAFETY

n. Efforts to prevent harm to patients during healthcare treatment. Commonly employed by hospitals, regulators, and quality improvement teams.

"Patient safety meant triple-checking everyone's name tag so we didn't prescribe foot cream to a patient needing heart surgery."

Related Terms: Care coordination, Value-based care, Chronic care management

PATIENT-CENTERED CARE

n. Healthcare focused on individual patient needs and preferences. Commonly employed by providers, insurers, and reform advocates.

"We embraced patient-centered care by asking patients which elevator music they preferred while waiting two hours."

Related Terms: Medical home, Integrated care, Value-based care

PEANUT BUTTER SPREAD

(Noun) Distributing resources, budget, or effort evenly across projects or departments, rather than focusing on priority areas—like smearing mediocre results everywhere. Commonly employed by cautious managers and committees avoiding tough choices.

"Our peanut butter spread strategy ensured everyone got a slice of funds, but no one got enough to matter."

Related Terms: Low-hanging fruit, Busy work, Make hay

PEER-TO-PEER FUNDRAISING

n. Supporters raising money for a nonprofit by engaging their personal networks. Commonly employed by nonprofits, charities, and donors seeking broader involvement.

"Our peer-to-peer fundraising depended on guilting friends into donating, proving friendship can be monetized."

Related Terms: Crowdfunding, Fundraising campaign, Donor stewardship

PEER-TO-PEER LENDING

n. Lending money directly between individuals via online platforms, bypassing banks. Commonly employed by fintech firms, investors, and borrowers.

"Peer-to-peer lending felt like borrowing from a neighbor, except the neighbor wanted interest and a credit check."

Related Terms: DeFi (Decentralized Finance), Crypto wallet, FinTech (Financial Technology)

PENCIL IN

v. To tentatively schedule something, subject to confirmation. Commonly employed by assistants, managers, and colleagues arranging calendars.

"They said 'pencil it in,' meaning we'd erase it later when something more urgent popped up."

Related Terms: DNB (Do Not Bother/Book), EOD (End Of Day), Cadence

PENCIL PUSHER

n. Someone performing dull, bureaucratic tasks, often with little creativity. Commonly employed by coworkers and critics mocking administrative roles.

"The pencil pusher spent hours filing reports that would never see daylight, living the dream of monotony."

Related Terms: Busy work, Donkey work, Just filling seats

PENNY WISE, POUND FOOLISH

phrase. Saving small amounts while ignoring bigger, more impactful costs. Commonly employed by critics noting misguided frugality.

"We saved a few bucks on office snacks, but lost thousands in productivity—truly penny wise, pound foolish."

Related Terms: Cost-benefit analysis, Scope creep, Lean waste

PENSION FUND MANAGEMENT

n. Managing and investing pension funds for future payouts. Commonly employed by CFOs, HR, and fund managers ensuring employee retirement security.

"Our pension fund management strategy resembled tossing darts at a Wall Street ticker and hoping for the best."

Related Terms: Fiscal responsibility, Due diligence, Investment property

PENSION REFORM

n. Changes to pension systems aimed at ensuring long-term sustainability. Commonly employed by policymakers, economists, and governments tackling aging populations.

"Pension reform was discussed as if we could turn decades of financial neglect into solvency overnight."

Related Terms: Fiscal policy, Economic stimulus, Fiscal responsibility

PERFECTION PARALYSIS

n. Failing to complete something because it's not perfect. Commonly employed by managers, designers, and creatives warning against over-polishing.

"We sank into perfection paralysis, polishing slide decks until deadlines passed and slides turned to dust."

Related Terms: MVP (Minimum Viable Product), Iterate, Knee-jerk reactions

PHILANTHROPY

n. Donating money or resources to causes promoting welfare. Commonly employed by foundations, donors, and charitable organizations.

"Our philanthropy matched every dollar donated with a shrug and a pat on the back—charity at its finest."

Related Terms: Charitable giving, CSR (Corporate social responsibility), Impact investing

PHYSICIAN ASSISTANT (PA)

n. A healthcare professional practicing under a physician's supervision, performing exams and writing prescriptions. Commonly employed by clinics, hospitals, and medical practices.

"Our PA handled most patient questions while the doctor hid behind charts—teamwork!"

Related Terms: Care coordination, Chronic care management, Value-based care

PICK YOUR BRAIN

phrase. To solicit someone's ideas or opinions on a topic. Commonly employed by managers, colleagues, and collaborators seeking input.

"They said they wanted to pick my brain, and I hoped they'd at least leave a few functioning cells."

Related Terms: Chime in, Brain dump, Ideate

PIE IN THE SKY

phrase. An unrealistic or overly optimistic idea or promise. Commonly employed by skeptics, analysts, and team members noting impractical dreams.

"Our CEO's vision of dominating the galaxy's markets was pure pie in the sky—delicious, but not edible."

Related Terms: Panacea, Magic bullet, Overpromise, underdeliver

PIGGYBACKING

v. Using someone else's work, success, or momentum for one's own benefit. Commonly employed by employees, opportunists, and competitors riding coattails.

"We piggybacked on a viral meme, attempting to appear hip before promptly falling off and breaking our dignity."

Related Terms: Cutthroat, Milk, Playing politics

PING ME

(Phrase) A request to message, call, or otherwise contact someone, typically in digital form, as if "email me" or "call me" is too old-school. Commonly employed by colleagues, managers, and teams trying to sound hip and tech-savvy.

"Just ping me with those numbers, because saying 'send me an email' apparently isn't cool anymore."

Related Terms: Circle back, In the loop, Offline

PITCH DECK

n. A presentation used by startups to inform and attract potential investors. Commonly employed by entrepreneurs, founders, and VCs reviewing opportunities.

"Our pitch deck had more buzzwords than meaningful stats, hoping investors would invest before waking from the trance."

Related Terms: Go to market, A/B testing, Innovation

PITCHING

v. Presenting an idea, product, or service to gain support or funding. Commonly employed by sales teams, founders, and business developers.

"We spent weeks pitching to investors, only to realize we were just adding them to our spam contact list."

Related Terms: Pitch deck, Go-to-market strategy, Conversion rate

PIVOT

v. To significantly change strategy, direction, or focus in response to market feedback or challenges. Commonly employed by startups, product managers, and business strategists.

"We pivoted so often our business plan resembled a merry-go-round that never stopped spinning."

Related Terms: Lean startup, Iterate, Disruption

PLAYING POLITICS

v. Using manipulative tactics or alliances for personal gain, often at others' expense. Commonly employed by employees, observers, and critics describing office intrigue.

"Playing politics turned our team into a soap opera, minus the glamour and with more memos."

Related Terms: Malicious obedience, HiPPO (Highest-Paid Person's Opinion), Macromanager

PLAYING WHACK-A-MOLE

phrase. Dealing repeatedly with minor issues without addressing the root cause. Commonly employed by managers, employees, and IT teams stuck in reactive modes.

"Fixing bugs was like playing whack-a-mole, except the moles had PhDs in annoyance."

Related Terms: Knee-jerk reactions, Crisis mode, Flogging a dead horse

PLENARY

n. A meeting or session attended by all relevant stakeholders. Commonly employed by organizations, conferences, and committees requiring full participation.

"Our plenary session felt like a forced family reunion—lots of nodding, some yawning, and zero resolutions."

Related Terms: Consensus building, Stakeholder engagement, Chime in

POLICY ADVOCACY

n. Efforts to influence public policy decisions in a particular direction.

Commonly employed by nonprofits, lobbyists, and advocacy groups.

"Policy advocacy was just lobbying in a nicer suit, smiling while handing out reports nobody read."

Related Terms: Lobbying, Public policy, Government accountability

POLICY FRAMEWORK

n. A set of principles or guidelines forming the basis for policy decisions. Commonly employed by policymakers, analysts, and leaders to structure governance.

"Our policy framework included rules so vague they might as well have said, 'Do good stuff, try hard.'"

Related Terms: Public policy, Regulatory compliance, Chatham House Rules

POLICY LOOPHOLE

n. A gap or ambiguity in regulations that can be exploited. Commonly employed by lawyers, lobbyists, and opportunists.

"We exploited a policy loophole so obvious it was like a billboard reading 'Free shortcut here!'"

Related Terms: Regulatory compliance, Bureaucratic red tape, Resistance to change

POLICY MISALIGNMENT

n. When government policies conflict with each other, causing inefficiencies. Commonly employed by policy analysts, critics, and reformers.

"Policy misalignment made our environmental program cut down trees to print sustainability pamphlets—brilliant."

Related Terms: Intergovernmental relations, Government accountability, Bureaucratic inefficiency

POPULATION HEALTH

n. The health outcomes of a group, including the distribution of outcomes. Commonly employed by public health professionals, policymakers, and healthcare administrators.

"Studying population health reminded us that collectively, we're as healthy as a candy store's clientele."

Related Terms: Value-based care, Chronic care management, Public policy

PORK BARREL SPENDING

n. Government funds allocated for local projects to gain political support rather than public benefit. Commonly employed by critics, media, and watchdogs highlighting wasteful spending.

"Our city's pork barrel spending went to a gold-plated gazebo—because what good is tax money if not spent on shiny nonsense?"

Related Terms: Pork-barrel project, Public policy, Fiscal policy

PORK-BARREL PROJECT

n. A project funded for political reasons rather than actual need or value. Commonly employed by critics and taxpayers frustrated with wasteful government expenditures.

"They built a museum of paperclips as a pork-barrel project, proving that not all museums deserve visitors."

Related Terms: Pork barrel spending, Policy misalignment, Bureaucratic red tape

PRESSURE TEST

v. Evaluating a plan to identify weaknesses before implementation. Commonly employed by project managers, strategists, and advisors ensuring robustness.

"We pressure tested our idea by asking tough questions, only to watch it collapse like a flan in a cupboard."

Related Terms: Due diligence, Deep dive, A/B testing

PREVENTIVE CARE

n. Healthcare services aimed at preventing disease rather than treating it after onset. Commonly employed by insurers, healthcare providers, and public health advocates.

"We encouraged preventive care, as it's cheaper to avoid a fire than rebuild the house after it burns down."

Related Terms: Value-based care, Care coordination, Chronic care management

PRIOR AUTHORIZATION

n. Approval required by health insurers before certain procedures or medications are covered. Commonly employed by insurers, providers, and patients navigating coverage.

"Getting prior authorization felt like asking a bouncer's permission to treat your own illness."

Related Terms: Fee-for-service, Capitation, Value-based care

PROCESS FATIGUE

n. Diminishing returns from applying the same process improvements repeatedly without fresh thinking. Commonly employed by Lean practitioners, managers, and operations teams.

"Our team suffered process fatigue, where every 'improvement' was as refreshing as a stale donut."

Related Terms: Lean methodology, Making sausage, Flogging a dead horse

PROCUREMENT INTEGRITY

n. Ensuring fairness, transparency, and honesty in government or organizational purchasing. Commonly employed by procurement officers, auditors, and compliance teams.

"Procurement integrity meant our bidding process was only slightly rigged instead of blatantly so."

Related Terms: Regulatory compliance, Government accountability, Policy framework

PRODUCT-MARKET FIT

n. When a product's features match market demand sufficiently for sustainable growth. Commonly employed by startups, product managers, and investors.

"We achieved product-market fit the moment customers stopped laughing at our app and started paying for it."

Related Terms: MVP (Minimum Viable Product), Market analysis, A/B testing

PRODUCTION LINE FAILURE

n. A breakdown or inefficiency in the manufacturing process, causing delays or defects. Commonly employed by operations managers, QA teams, and factory supervisors.

"Our production line failure sent us back to the drawing board—and by drawing board, I mean crying in the break room."

Related Terms: Bottleneck, Maintenance backlog, Lean waste

PROGRAM EVALUATION

n. Assessing the effectiveness and efficiency of a program or service. Commonly employed by nonprofits, evaluators, and grantmakers.

"Our program evaluation said we spent a fortune and achieved nothing—at least we got a fancy chart out of it."

Related Terms: Impact report, Case study, Cost-benefit analysis

PROGRAM IMPACT

n. The measurable outcomes or changes resulting from a program's activities. Commonly employed by nonprofits, CSR efforts, and philanthropic foundations.

"The program impact was so minimal we could've replaced the entire initiative with a motivational poster."

Related Terms: Impact report, Learnings, Case study

PROGRAM OFFICER

n. A professional managing specific programs or grants within a nonprofit or foundation. Commonly employed by philanthropic organizations, charities, and grantmakers.

"Our program officer juggled so many grants that we suspected they had extra arms hidden under their blazer."

Related Terms: Donor stewardship, Grant funding, Program evaluation

PROGRAMMATIC TV

n. Automating buying and selling of TV ad inventory similarly to programmatic digital ads. Commonly employed by advertisers, media buyers, and broadcasting networks.

"Programmatic TV promised efficient ad placement; we ended up with infomercials airing at midnight for insomniac penguins."

Related Terms: Programmatic advertising, Cross-channel marketing, A/B testing

PROGRAMMATIC ADVERTISING

n. Automated, data-driven buying and selling of online ad inventory. Commonly employed by digital marketers, ad tech companies, and media buyers.

"Programmatic advertising targeted my cat more accurately than me, suggesting Mittens might have interesting purchase history."

Related Terms: A/B testing, Conversion rate, Influencer marketing

PROGRAMMATIC DIRECT

n. Programmatically buying premium ad inventory at a fixed price without an auction. Commonly employed by advertisers and publishers seeking stable pricing.

"We went programmatic direct, locking in prices so stable it felt like buying bottled air at a set premium."

Related Terms: Programmatic advertising, Cross-channel marketing, CTR (Click-Through Rate)

PROGRAMMATIC FUNDING

n. Funding designated for a specific program or initiative within a nonprofit. Commonly employed by grantmakers, foundations, and nonprofits allocating resources.

"Our programmatic funding ensured we could only spend money on training volunteers to fold pamphlets, not actually help anyone."

Related Terms: Capital campaign, Grant funding, Program evaluation

PROPERTY MANAGEMENT

n. Overseeing and maintaining real estate properties, including tenant issues and repairs. Commonly employed by landlords, property managers, and real estate investors.

"Property management turned into referee work when tenants argued over who should clean the shared porch."

Related Terms: Investment property, Foreclosure, Lease agreement

PROTOTYPE

n. An early model of a product used for testing and feedback before full-scale production. Commonly employed by designers, engineers, and product teams.

"Our prototype was held together by duct tape and hope, a true testament to innovation under budget constraints."

Related Terms: MVP (Minimum Viable Product), A/B testing, Lean startup

PUBLIC ADMINISTRATION

n. Implementing and managing government policies, programs, and services. Commonly employed by civil servants, policymakers, and public sector managers.

"Public administration was less about serving the public and more about surviving endless forms and three-letter acronyms."

Related Terms: Public policy, Government accountability, Bureaucratic red tape

PUBLIC HEALTH EMERGENCY

n. A widespread threat to health requiring government intervention. Commonly employed by health officials, policymakers, and emergency management teams.

"The public health emergency revealed that we have more contingency plans for office birthdays than actual crises."

Related Terms: Population health, Preventive care, Public health policy

PUBLIC HEALTH POLICY

n. Government actions protecting and improving population health. Commonly employed by policymakers, health departments, and advocacy groups.

"Our public health policy pamphlet looked impressive, but we spent more time on its font than its measures."

Related Terms: Population health, Value-based care, Public policy

PUBLIC INTEREST LITIGATION

n. Legal actions taken to protect or advance public welfare. Commonly employed by advocates, legal nonprofits, and social justice groups.

"We filed public interest litigation hoping for justice, but the court schedule said, 'See you in three years.'"

Related Terms: Policy advocacy, FOIA (Freedom of information act), Government accountability

PUBLIC OPINION POLLING

n. Surveying the public to measure opinions on policies, politicians, or societal issues. Commonly employed by pollsters, politicians, and media outlets.

"Our public opinion polling said people love lower taxes, safer streets, and free ice cream—who knew?"

Related Terms: Public policy, Election integrity, Census data

PUBLIC POLICY

n. Government laws, regulations, and actions addressing societal issues. Commonly employed by policymakers, citizens, and lobbyists debating governance.

"Our public policy was so unclear that citizens treated it like an abstract art piece: everyone guessed what it meant."

Related Terms: Policy advocacy, Policy framework, Government accountability

PUBLIC SECTOR

n. The part of the economy controlled by the government. Commonly employed by economists, policymakers, and commentators.

"Working in the public sector felt like starring in a slow-motion documentary on red tape."

Related Terms: Public administration, Intergovernmental relations, Public sector reform

PUBLIC SECTOR REFORM

n. Efforts to improve efficiency and transparency in government services. Commonly employed by policymakers, watchdog groups, and reform advocates.

"Our public sector reform turned five-day processes into four-day processes—progress!"

Related Terms: Government accountability, Bureaucratic red tape, Policy misalignment

PUBLIC TRUST

n. The confidence citizens have in government integrity and competence. Commonly employed by policy analysts, media, and civic organizations.

"We tried to build public trust with a town hall meeting; we ended up with a shouting match and stale cookies."

Related Terms: Government accountability, Governmental transparency, Election integrity

PUBLIC-PRIVATE PARTNERSHIP (PPP)

n. A cooperative arrangement between government and the private sector. Commonly employed by policymakers, investors, and infrastructure planners.

"Our PPP tried to marry bureaucracy with corporate greed—a match made in efficiency heaven…not."

Related Terms: Public policy, Government procurement, Fiscal policy

PUNT

v. Postponing or avoiding a decision, passing responsibility to someone else. Commonly employed by managers, execs, and team leads deferring tough choices.

"We decided to punt the budget issue, hoping tomorrow's version of us would be braver or more caffeinated."

Related Terms: Circle back, Let it bake, Marinate

PUPPET SHOW

n. A situation where apparent decision-makers are actually controlled by others behind the scenes. Commonly employed by employees, critics, and observers noting hidden agendas.

"In our puppet show of a committee, the strings led back to an executive's office where laughter echoed."

Related Terms: Playing politics, Helicopter manager, HiPPO (Highest-Paid Person's Opinion)

PUSH BACK

v. To resist or object to a plan, proposal, or directive. Commonly employed by employees, stakeholders, and team members exercising dissent.

"We tried to push back on the 7 AM meeting, but were rewarded with a 6 AM meeting the next week."

Related Terms: Knee-jerk reactions, Resistance to change, Playing politics

PUSHING THE PANIC BUTTON

phrase. Overreacting to a situation instead of responding calmly. Commonly employed by employees, observers, and advisors noting panic-driven decisions.

"When sales dipped 1%, the CEO pushed the panic button so hard it broke, along with our morale."

Related Terms: Panic-driven decisions, Knee-jerk reactions, Crisis mode

PUSHING WET SPAGHETTI

phrase. Attempting to lead or manage something inherently unmanageable. Commonly employed humorously by managers, coaches, and team leads.

"Organizing the interns was like pushing wet spaghetti uphill—messy, pointless, and guaranteed to fail."

Related Terms: Herding cats, Herding turtles, Death march

PUT ON THE BACKBURNER

phrase. To deprioritize or delay action on a task or project. Commonly employed by managers, project leads, and colleagues deferring tasks.

"We put the redesign on the backburner so long it turned into a cold lump of abandoned pixels."

Related Terms: Marinate, Let it bake, Circle back

Q

IS FOR QUICK WINS BECAUSE QUICK WINS QUELL QUARRELS AND QUIETLY QUALIFY OUR QUEST FOR QUALITY.

QC (QUALITY CONTROL)

abbr. + n. A process to ensure there are no defects in products or services before delivery. Commonly employed by manufacturing lines, QA teams, and quality managers.

"Our QC process caught so many errors that we wondered if the product was just an elaborate prank on our customers."

Related Terms: Quality control failure, Lean methodology, Bottleneck

QBR (QUARTERLY BUSINESS REVIEW)

(Abbreviation) A periodic meeting, often quarterly, where performance, strategy, and results are assessed to ensure alignment with goals. Commonly employed by sales teams, account managers, and executives evaluating client relationships or internal metrics.

"Our QBR turned into a parade of spreadsheets, but at least we pretended to care."

Related Terms: Key takeaway, Executive summary, High level

QUALIFIED LEADS

(Noun) Potential customers who meet certain criteria indicating higher likelihood of purchasing, often used to prioritize sales efforts. Commonly employed by marketing, sales teams, and demand generation strategists.

"We chased so many unqualified leads that finding a single qualified lead felt like striking gold."

Related Terms: Lead generation, Conversion rate, Churn

QUALITY ASSURANCE (QA)

(Noun) Processes designed to prevent defects and ensure a product or service meets certain standards. Commonly employed by QA teams, product managers, and engineers striving for reliability.

"Our quality assurance checks caught so many errors we wondered if we'd built anything right."

Related Terms: Deep dive, Lean methodology, Due diligence

QUALITY CIRCLE

(Noun) A group of employees who meet regularly to discuss work improvements, productivity boosts, and quality enhancements. Commonly employed by operations, manufacturing floors, and teams following Lean principles.

"Our quality circle spent two hours debating pen colors—true dedication to improvement."

Related Terms: Consensus building, Kaizen (not listed, but could be), Continuous improvement

QUALITY CONTROL FAILURE

n. When inadequate quality measures lead to defective products reaching consumers. Commonly employed by product teams, QA, and customers discovering poor quality.

"Our quality control failure meant customers received soda cans filled with flavored 'oops,' shaking confidence and taste buds alike."

Related Terms: QC (Quality Control), Broken workflow, Over-engineering

QUALITY-DRIVEN

(Adj.) Emphasizing excellence, precision, and standards as core priorities in processes or products. Commonly employed by leaders, project managers, and branding teams selling trust over speed.

"We claimed to be quality-driven, then outsourced half the work to a discount vendor."

Related Terms: Core competencies, Value proposition, Mission statement

QUANT JOCKEY

(Noun) A data-driven analyst or finance specialist who obsessively crunches numbers, models probabilities, and relies heavily on quantitative methods. Commonly employed by investment firms, trading desks, and analytics teams where metrics and spreadsheets rule decision-making.

"Our quant jockey generated so many charts that even the pie charts felt dizzy."

Related Terms: Quants, Machine learning, Data-driven

QUANTUM LEAP

(Phrase) A significant, substantial improvement or major advancement in performance or results. Commonly employed by motivational speakers, execs, and strategists hyping dramatic changes.

"They promised a quantum leap in productivity, which turned out to be a baby step wearing big shoes."

Related Terms: Game changer, Disruption, Moonshot Division

QUARTER / Q

n. A three-month period used in financial reporting. Commonly employed by accountants, CFOs, and investors tracking performance.

"In Q3, we measured success in how many crises we dodged rather than any sane metric."

Related Terms: Fiscal policy, ROI (Return on Investment), Burn rate

QUORUM

(Noun) The minimum number of members or participants required to conduct official business or decisions. Commonly employed by boards, committees, and formal groups ensuring meetings aren't just coffee breaks.

"Without a quorum, our grand plans fizzled, leaving us to contemplate empty chairs."

Related Terms: Consensus building, Plenary, Committee

QUEUE MANAGEMENT

(Noun) The process of controlling and organizing the order and flow of work tasks, customers, or data. Commonly employed by operations, IT support, and logistics teams wanting to avoid chaos.

"With proper queue management, we stopped treating tickets like confetti in a wind tunnel."

Related Terms: Bottleneck, Workflow, Cadence

QUICK AND DIRTY

(Adj.) A solution or approach done rapidly with minimal refinement, valuing speed over perfection. Commonly employed by developers, product managers, and teams racing against tight deadlines.

"We delivered a quick and dirty mockup—ugly, but it got the boss off our backs for the weekend."

Related Terms: Band-aid solution, Hack (if it existed), Donkey work

QUICK RATIO

(Noun) A financial metric measuring a company's short-term liquidity, showing how easily it can meet immediate obligations. Commonly employed by CFOs, investors, and analysts evaluating solvency without selling assets.

"Our quick ratio improved slightly after we stopped buying monogrammed staplers."

Related Terms: NOI, Burn rate, Fiscal responsibility

QUICK WIN

(Noun) A straightforward, easily achieved victory that provides immediate positive results. Commonly employed by managers, project leads, and efficiency experts demonstrating progress fast.

"We nailed a quick win by fixing that broken link—our highlight of the quarter."

Related Terms: Low-hanging fruit, Move the needle, Deep dive

QUARTERLY CADENCE

(Noun) A schedule or rhythm set every three months, often for reporting, reviews, or product releases. Commonly employed by planners, executives, and sales teams wanting regular check-ins.

"Our quarterly cadence ensured we panicked about deadlines like clockwork."

Related Terms: EOD/EOW, QBR, High level

QUERY OPTIMIZATION

(Noun) Improving search or database queries to run faster and use fewer resources. Commonly employed by IT, data analysts, and developers needing quick data access.

"After query optimization, our dashboard stopped loading at the speed of continental drift."

Related Terms: Data management platform (DMP), Analytics, Deep dive

QUID PRO QUO

(Noun) An exchange of goods or services where each party provides something of value. Commonly employed by negotiators, sales teams, and sometimes questionable leaders striking deals.

"Our partnership was pure quid pro quo—give us leads, we'll give you discounts."

Related Terms: Buy-in, Consensus building, In the loop

QUIET QUITTING

(Noun) The practice of doing the bare minimum at work, declining extra responsi-

bilities without explicitly resigning. Commonly employed by employees weary of burnout, HR execs anxious about morale.

"After months of overtime, she embraced quiet quitting—her tasks got done, no bonus strings attached."

Related Terms: Workstream, Dead weight, Donkey work

QUALIFYING QUESTIONS

(Noun) Specific inquiries used to determine if a lead, project, or partner meets criteria before investing effort. Commonly employed by sales teams, recruiters, and project managers screening prospects.

"We bombarded the prospect with qualifying questions until they fled—guess they weren't a match."

Related Terms: Qualified leads, Due diligence, Buy-in

QUALITY GATE

(Noun) A checkpoint in a process ensuring minimum standards are met before moving forward. Commonly employed by QA teams, developers, and project managers maintaining consistent standards.

"We hit the quality gate—barely—like a limbo champ scraping the bar."

Related Terms: Quality assurance, Lean methodology, Critical path

QUALITY FUNCTION DEPLOYMENT (QFD)

(Abbreviation) A method translating customer requirements into product specifications, ensuring design meets user needs. Commonly employed by product designers, engineers, and quality teams bridging desire and delivery.

"Our QFD exercise revealed customers wanted fewer features, not another useless bell."

Related Terms: Value proposition, Core competencies, User experience (UX)

QUANTITATIVE METRICS

(Noun) Measurable, numeric indicators of performance or progress, as opposed to qualitative measures. Commonly employed by analysts, CFOs, and results-obsessed managers.

"Our quantitative metrics showed growth, though we still felt like hamsters in a wheel."

Related Terms: Key Performance Indicator (KPI), Conversion rate, Data management platform (DMP)

QUANTS

(Noun) Individuals who specialize in quantitative analysis, often in finance,

crunching numbers at dizzying speeds. Commonly employed by investment firms, analysts, and modeling teams who worship spreadsheets.

"The quants crunched numbers so complex they made normal math look like finger painting."

Related Terms: Machine learning, Deep dive, Data-driven

QUOTA

(Noun) A set target or limit that must be met or not exceeded, often used in sales, production, or hiring. Commonly employed by managers, sales directors, and HR setting expectations.

"We hit our sales quota five minutes before close—pure luck, but who's asking?"

Related Terms: Key takeaway, Benchmark, High level

R

IS FOR ROI BECAUSE REAPING RICH REWARDS REQUIRES RIGOROUS ROI REVIEW— REVENUE REIGNS!

REIT (REAL ESTATE INVESTMENT TRUST)

abbr. + n. A company owning or financing income-producing real estate, allowing investors to buy shares. Commonly employed by investors, analysts, and portfolio managers.

"Investing in a REIT meant trusting someone else to pick properties, praying they don't buy haunted condos."

Related Terms: Cap rate (Capitalization rate), 1031 exchange, Investment property

RFP (REQUEST FOR PROPOSAL)

abbr. + n. A document soliciting bids or proposals for a specific project from potential suppliers. Commonly employed by procurement, project managers, and clients seeking the best vendor.

"Our RFP read like a riddle wrapped in legalese—vendors guessed what we wanted and we pretended to know the difference."

Related Terms: Procurement integrity, Cost-benefit analysis, Government procurement

ROI (RETURN ON INVESTMENT)

abbr. + n. A performance metric evaluating the profitability of an investment. Commonly employed by investors, CFOs, and managers justifying expenditures.

"Our ROI calculation suggested we'd be richer burning money for warmth—at least it's a controlled fire."

Related Terms: Cost-benefit analysis, KPI (Key Performance Indicator), Gain traction

RTB (REAL-TIME BIDDING)

abbr. + n. Buying and selling online ad impressions in auctions occurring as a webpage loads. Commonly employed by advertisers, ad tech companies, and digital marketers.

"RTB turned advertising into a chaotic stock exchange for eyeballs, where everyone shouts and no one listens."

Related Terms: Programmatic advertising, Conversion rate, A/B testing

REACH OUT

v. To contact or communicate with someone. Commonly employed by colleagues, managers, and customers seeking help or information.

"'Feel free to reach out' often means 'I dare you to email me so I can ignore it with style.'"

Related Terms: Loop in, Chime in, In the loop

REAL ESTATE AGENT COMMISSION

n. The fee paid to a real estate agent for facilitating a property transaction. Commonly employed by homebuyers, sellers, and agents.

"The agent's commission felt like a tip for doing what online listings could do—except this tip cost thousands."

Related Terms: Listing agent, Investment property, Real estate closing

REAL ESTATE BUBBLE

n. A market condition where property prices far exceed intrinsic value, risking a sudden drop. Commonly employed by analysts, economists, and investors warning about overvaluation.

"We rode the real estate bubble until it popped and left our portfolio as empty as a freshly evicted condo."

Related Terms: Cap rate (Capitalization rate), Foreclosure, Investment property

REAL ESTATE CLOSING

n. The final step in a property transaction, transferring ownership. Commonly employed by buyers, sellers, lawyers, and real estate agents.

"The closing took so long we expected the notary to ask for birthday cake before handing over the keys."

Related Terms: Foreclosure, Investment property, Escrow

REAL ESTATE CROWDFUNDING

n. Pooling funds from multiple individuals online to finance a real estate project. Commonly employed by startups, investors, and platforms democratizing investment.

"Real estate crowdfunding felt like passing the hat around for a building—just with more zeros and legal disclaimers."

Related Terms: Crowdfunding, REIT (Real Estate Investment Trust), Cap rate (Capitalization rate)

REAL ESTATE DEVELOPMENT

n. Purchasing, improving, and selling properties for profit. Commonly employed by developers, investors, and urban planners.

"Our foray into real estate development ended with a half-built mall and a fully-built regret complex."

Related Terms: Greenfield site, Brownfield site, Cap rate (Capitalization rate)

REAL ESTATE SYNDICATION

n. A partnership pooling money from multiple investors to buy larger real estate projects. Commonly employed by investors, developers, and deal sponsors.

"In real estate syndication, we joined strangers in hoping a building appreciates instead of depreciates into tears."

Related Terms: REIT (Real Estate Investment Trust), Crowdfunding, Investment property

REAL-TIME MARKETING

n. Delivering marketing messages immediately in response to current events or trends.

Commonly employed by social media teams, brands, and marketers capitalizing on moments.

"Our real-time marketing responded to a trending meme so fast that by the time we posted, the meme had died."

Related Terms: Cross-channel marketing, A/B testing, Programmatic advertising

REARRANGING DECK CHAIRS

phrase. Making superficial changes that don't address core problems. Commonly employed by employees, critics, and analysts mocking futile efforts.

"We kept rearranging deck chairs on this sinking project, impressing no one except the ship's ghost."

Related Terms: Flogging a dead horse, Bubble mentality, Groundhog Day

RED OCEAN (OR 'BLUE OCEAN')

n. Red ocean: saturated, competitive markets; Blue ocean: new, uncontested markets. Commonly employed by strategists, marketers, and entrepreneurs seeking growth.

"We aimed for a blue ocean but ended up in a red ocean, swimming with sharks who had MBAs."

Related Terms: Disruption, Innovation, Go to market

RED TAPE

n. Excessive bureaucracy or adherence to formalities slowing down decisions. Commonly employed by employees, managers, and critics describing procedural barriers.

"Drowning in red tape, we developed gills of compliance and fins of acceptance."

Related Terms: Bureaucratic inefficiency, Government accountability, Public sector reform

REDUNDANT SYSTEMS

n. Unnecessary duplicates providing the same function, causing inefficiency. Commonly employed by IT, operations, and process improvement specialists.

"Our redundant systems meant we had backups for backups, ensuring double the headaches for half the efficiency."

Related Terms: Lean waste, Over-engineering, Broken workflow

REGIONAL DEVELOPMENT

n. Programs promoting economic growth and infrastructure improvements in specific areas. Commonly employed by policymakers, planners, and community stakeholders.

"Regional development sounded great until we realized we were developing regions into theme parks of paperwork."

Related Terms: Public policy, Economic stimulus, Intergovernmental relations

REGULATORY CAPTURE

n. When regulatory agencies are dominated by the industries they're supposed to regulate. Commonly employed by critics, economists, and watchdogs describing compromised oversight.

"Regulatory capture explained why the watchdog nodded off while the fox strolled into the henhouse."

Related Terms: Lobbying, Government accountability, Policy advocacy

REGULATORY COMPLIANCE

n. Adhering to laws, regulations, and standards set by authorities. Commonly employed by compliance officers, legal teams, and managers ensuring adherence.

"We achieved regulatory compliance by turning our policies into bedtime reading for insomniacs."

Related Terms: Procurement integrity, Due diligence, Mandate

REGULATORY SANDBOX

n. A controlled environment for testing new policies or products without full regulatory constraints. Commonly employed by policymakers, innovators, and startups experimenting safely.

"In the regulatory sandbox, we played with new ideas like toddlers building sandcastles of maybe-success."

Related Terms: Innovation, DeFi (Decentralized Finance), Lean startup

REINVENT THE WHEEL

phrase. Redoing something unnecessarily instead of using existing solutions. Commonly employed by managers, colleagues, and advisors urging efficiency.

"We reinvented the wheel so many times it turned square, then triangle, then just collapsed."

Related Terms: Cookie-cutter approach, Flogging a dead horse, Scope creep

RESISTANCE TO CHANGE

n. Reluctance or refusal to adapt to new methods or processes. Commonly employed by managers, change agents, and consultants overcoming inertia.

"Our resistance to change meant we clung to outdated software like a security blanket made of glitches."

Related Terms: Lack of vision, Silo mentality, Playing politics

RESONATE

v. To connect with someone's preferences or leave a meaningful impression. Commonly employed by marketers, communicators, and designers testing impact.

"Our heartfelt mission statement was supposed to resonate with employees, but it echoed like a bad joke in an empty room."

Related Terms: Client-centric, Customer journey, Key takeaway

RESTRICTED FUNDS

n. Donations or grants given to a nonprofit with specific conditions on usage. Commonly employed by nonprofits, charities, and foundations tracking money flow.

"Our restricted funds could only pay for pamphlets about pamphlets, truly a noble use of resources."

Related Terms: Capital campaign, Donor stewardship, Programmatic funding

RETAIL SPACE LEASING

n. Renting out commercial spaces to businesses selling goods or services. Commonly employed by landlords, property managers, and retailers expanding locations.

"We tried retail space leasing, but the only taker was a store selling upcycled socks—a niche market indeed."

Related Terms: Property management, Investment property, Real estate development

RETARGETING

n. Displaying ads to users who previously interacted with a brand. Commonly employed by marketers, advertisers, and digital media buyers.

"After I viewed one blender, retargeting followed me around the internet, offering blender deals until I questioned my existence."

Related Terms: Programmatic advertising, A/B testing, Conversion rate

REVENUE

n. Income earned by an organization through its operations. Commonly employed by CFOs, investors, and business owners tracking financial health.

"Our revenue soared once we stopped chasing 'strategic visions' and started charging people actual money."

Related Terms: ROI (Return on Investment), Cap rate (Capitalization rate), Cost-benefit analysis

REVERSE ENGINEER

v. To deconstruct something to understand how it was created. Commonly employed by engineers, analysts, and curious competitors.

"We tried to reverse engineer our competitor's success and ended up copying their packaging tape—progress?"

Related Terms: Deep dive, Due diligence, Flesh out

RIDING THE COATTAILS

phrase. Benefiting from someone else's success or efforts without contributing. Commonly employed by colleagues, critics, and observers noting freeloading behavior.

"We rode the CEO's coattails so shamelessly he considered wearing a shorter jacket."

Related Terms: Piggybacking, Playing politics, Cutthroat

RISK MANAGEMENT

n. Identifying, assessing, and controlling risks to minimize harm and improve safety. Commonly employed by compliance teams, project managers, and insurance companies.

"Our risk management plan involved hoping bad things wouldn't happen and acting surprised when they did."

Related Terms: Due diligence, Crisis management, Cost-benefit analysis

ROADMAP

n. A strategic plan outlining future steps, milestones, and timelines for a project or product. Commonly employed by product managers, project leads, and executives.

"Our product roadmap was so vague it looked more like a kid's treasure map, complete with 'X marks the spot' confusion."

Related Terms: Go-to-market strategy, Iterate, Marinate

ROBO-ADVISOR

n. An automated platform providing algorithm-driven financial planning services. Commonly employed by investors, fintech platforms, and advisors automating advice.

"The robo-advisor suggested investing in 'Stable Unicorns Inc.,' confirming even robots have a sense of humor."

Related Terms: FinTech (Financial Technology), DeFi (Decentralized Finance), Risk management

ROBUST

adj. Describing something capable of enduring challenges without breaking down. Commonly employed by product developers, IT staff, and engineers praising durability.

"Our system was so robust that only half of it crashed under peak load, a win by our standards."

Related Terms: Scalable, Lean methodology, Innovation

ROCKET SCIENCE

phrase. A metaphor for something highly complex or difficult to understand. Commonly employed by managers, team members, and critics downplaying complexity.

"They said mastering our CRM wasn't rocket science, which is true—rocket science might be easier."

Related Terms: Deep dive, Counterfactual, Granular

ROCKSTAR

n. A term for a highly skilled or outstanding individual in a field. Commonly employed by recruiters, managers, and colleagues praising top performers.

"We called him a rockstar developer, but all he did was play air guitar with the code and ship bugs."

Related Terms: Aces in their places, Core competency, Meritocracy

RUBBER STAMP

n. Automatically approving decisions without proper consideration. Commonly employed by boards, committees, and leadership under weak governance.

"Our board was a rubber stamp; suggest anything and watch those stamps go thunk-thunk with no questions asked."

Related Terms: HiPPO (Highest-Paid Person's Opinion), Empty suit, Overpromise, underdeliver

RUNNING ON FUMES

phrase. Continuing to work despite being completely exhausted or out of resources. Commonly employed by employees, teams, and managers nearing burnout.

"By Friday, we were running on fumes and stale coffee, high-fiving the concept of sleep from afar."

Related Terms: Burnout, Busy work, Hostage mentality

S

IS FOR SYNERGY BECAUSE SYNERGY SOUNDS SLICK, STIMULATING SHARED SUCCESS —SURELY SHIMMERING SHORTHAND!

S.W.A.T. TEAM

n. A specialized group assembled to tackle urgent tasks or problems. Commonly employed by project leads, executives, and crisis managers.

"Our S.W.A.T. team addressed crises by circling them menacingly, then writing stern emails."

Related Terms: Crisis management, Failover failure, Risk management

SME (SUBJECT MATTER EXPERT)

abbr. + n. A person with deep knowledge in a particular field or topic. Commonly employed by project managers, consultants, and interviewers seeking expert input.

"We asked the SME for input, and they dazzled us with jargon until we nodded politely, none the wiser."

Related Terms: Aces in their places, Core competency, Green

SOW (SCOPE OF WORK)

abbr. + n. A document defining project deliverables, timelines, and responsibilities. Commonly employed by project managers, clients, and vendors.

"Our SOW was so detailed it felt like reading a legal thriller, minus the thrill."

Related Terms: Scope, Deliverables, Due diligence

SPOC (SINGLE POINT OF CONTACT)

abbr. + n. The main individual to communicate with regarding a project or relationship. Commonly employed by managers, clients, and collaborators centralizing communication.

"Our SPOC vanished into witness protection, leaving us to guess who to bother next."

Related Terms: POC (Point Of Contact), Loop in, In the loop

SSSD (SAME SHIT SAME DAY)

abbr. + phrase. Slang indicating repetitive tasks or unchanging circumstances. Commonly employed informally by employees stuck in monotony.

"At our office, SSSD was practically the slogan, reminding us that variety is overrated."

Related Terms: Groundhog Day, Busy work, Mediocrity

SWOT ANALYSIS (STRENGTHS, WEAKNESSES, OPPORTUNITIES, THREATS)

n. A strategic planning tool assessing a project or company from multiple angles. Commonly employed by strategists, consultants, and managers making informed decisions.

"Our SWOT analysis revealed strengths (we exist), weaknesses (we struggle), opportunities (slim), and threats (everything else)."

Related Terms: Cost-benefit analysis, Deep dive, Key takeaway

SAAS (SOFTWARE AS A SERVICE)

abbr. + n. Cloud-based software delivered on a subscription basis. Commonly employed by tech companies, IT departments, and software users.

"We launched a SaaS product promising convenience; users got convenience if they conveniently ignored the glitches."

Related Terms: Cloud computing, Conversion rate, MVP (Minimum Viable Product)

SANDBOX

n. A safe environment for testing ideas, systems, or code without real consequences. Commonly employed by developers, innovators, and pilots of new initiatives.

"We played in the sandbox of innovation and built a sandcastle of hope, which promptly collapsed."

Related Terms: Regulatory sandbox, Lean startup, Prototype

SAVE UP

v. To store or preserve a document under a new version or date for future use. Commonly employed by archivists, careful editors, and version-control advocates.

"We saved up so many file versions that our hard drive turned into a museum of indecision."

Related Terms: Hard copy, Paper, Due diligence

SCALABILITY

n. The ability of a system or process to handle growth without performance loss. Commonly employed by startups, tech companies, and strategists planning expansion.

"Our product's scalability was so questionable it panicked at the thought of new users."

Related Terms: Scalable, Lean methodology, Digital transformation

SCALABILITY ISSUES

n. Problems arising when a product or process cannot handle increased demand efficiently. Commonly employed by startups, IT teams, and operations managers.

"We faced scalability issues so severe that adding one user felt like adding a thousand elephants to a teetering seesaw."

Related Terms: Scalability, Over-engineering, Bottleneck

SCALABLE

adj. Capable of handling increased demand or growth efficiently. Commonly employed by startups, tech companies, and business strategists.

"We called our solution scalable, meaning we hoped it wouldn't collapse into a dramatic meltdown when users arrived."

Related Terms: Scalability, Lean startup, Gain traction

SCARLET LETTER

n. A symbol of shame or public disgrace. Commonly employed by employees, commentators, and critics describing branding failures.

"After the product flopped, its logo became our scarlet letter, haunting our PowerPoints."

Related Terms: Dumpster fire, Death spiral, Overpromise, underdeliver

SCOOBY SNACKS

n. Small rewards or tokens of appreciation. Commonly employed informally by managers and colleagues trying to boost morale cheaply.

"We offered Scooby Snacks—cheap candy and forced smiles—as a morale booster. Shockingly, morale didn't soar."

Related Terms: Quick win, Busy work, Donkey work

SCOPE

n. The defined boundaries and deliverables of a project. Commonly employed by project managers, clients, and stakeholders setting expectations.

"Our project scope was so vague we suspected the manager read it in a foggy crystal ball."

Related Terms: SOW (Scope Of Work), Deliverables, Scope creep

SCOPE CREEP

n. The tendency for a project's scope to expand beyond the original plan. Commonly employed by project managers, clients, and teams warning against uncontrolled changes.

"Scope creep turned a simple webpage update into a full-on website redesign plus a new company anthem."

Related Terms: SOW (Scope Of Work), Flogging a dead horse, Reinvent the wheel

SCREAMING INTO THE VOID

phrase. Expressing frustration or ideas with no one listening or responding. Commonly employed by employees, customers, or users feeling ignored.

"Providing feedback here is like screaming into the void—echoes of indifference are all we get."

Related Terms: Groundhog Day, In the weeds, Mushroom principle

SCREW THE POOCH

phrase. To make a major mistake or mishandle a situation badly. Commonly employed informally by team members, employees, and friends noting a big blunder.

"We screwed the pooch by shipping a broken feature, turning our release party into a pity party."

Related Terms: Knee-jerk reactions, Dumpster fire, Burning bridges

SCRUB

n. An entry-level, easily replaceable employee, often used derogatorily. Commonly employed jokingly or insultingly by coworkers or managers.

"They treated the new hire like a scrub, assigning tedious tasks that bored even the office plants."

Related Terms: Donkey work, Busy work, Just filling seats

SCUTTLEBUTT

n. Gossip or rumors circulating within a group. Commonly employed by employees, sailors (historically), and colleagues sharing informal intel.

"The scuttlebutt around the water cooler claimed our CEO was considering stand-up comedy, which explained a lot."

Related Terms: Bullshit bingo, Bubble mentality, Meanderthal

SEA LEGS

n. Becoming stable or comfortable in a new situation, especially a challenging one. Commonly employed by managers, mentors, and team leads encouraging adaptation.

"We got our sea legs after a month of nonstop confusion, now we're just regularly confused instead of panicked."

Related Terms: Green, Heads down, Burnout

SEAMLESS

adj. Operating so smoothly that transitions or boundaries aren't noticeable. Commonly employed by product designers, IT teams, and service providers.

"Our 'seamless' integration crashed three times, proving that sometimes seams are necessary."

Related Terms: Robust, Customer-centric, Cloud-based

SECOND COMING

n. A reemergence or revival of something once considered failed. Commonly employed by marketers, executives, and teams relaunching products.

"They called the product's relaunch our 'second coming,' but the public yawned like it was a second helping of failure."

Related Terms: Pivot, Go to market, Groundhog Day

SECURITY THEATER

n. Visible security measures creating a false sense of safety without real protection. Commonly employed by critics, employees, and observers noting pointless checks.

"Our security theater included badge checks and stern looks, stopping no one but well-meaning interns."

Related Terms: Chatham House Rules, Red tape, Bubble mentality

SEED ROUND

n. Initial funding raised by a startup to begin developing a product or idea. Commonly employed by entrepreneurs, VCs, and angel investors.

"After our seed round, we had just enough cash to buy coffee and pretend we were building the next unicorn."

Related Terms: MVP (Minimum Viable Product), A/B testing, Lean startup

SEGMENT

v. To categorize or organize data or users into groups for analysis or targeting. Commonly employed by marketers, analysts, and product teams.

"We segmented our audience into groups: 'fickle,' 'bored,' and 'easily bribed with discounts.'"

Related Terms: A/B testing, Conversion rate, Contextual targeting

SENSE CHECK

v. Quickly reviewing if something is logical or reasonable. Commonly employed by managers, analysts, and colleagues ensuring no glaring flaws.

"Let's sense check this forecast; if we sell more units than there are people on Earth, maybe we need to rethink."

Related Terms: Cost-benefit analysis, Deep dive, Due diligence

SERIAL ENTREPRENEUR

n. An individual who starts multiple businesses, not all of which may succeed. Commonly employed by investors, media, and startup communities.

"Our serial entrepreneur founded a dozen startups; some flopped so hard they're still leaving crater marks."

Related Terms: Lean startup, FinTech (Financial Technology), Disruption

SERIES A

n. A startup's first major round of institutional funding for growth beyond the seed stage. Commonly employed by founders, VCs, and startup accelerators.

"At Series A, we sold investors on dreams and metrics so vague they resembled poetry."

Related Terms: Seed round, MVP (Minimum Viable Product), Product-market fit

SERIES B

n. A later financing round for a startup that has met certain milestones post-Series A. Commonly employed by founders, investors, and startup watchers tracking growth stages.

"Series B meant we proved we're still alive and maybe even doing something right—investors cheered softly."

Related Terms: Series A, Growth hacking, Go-to-market strategy

SERVING SUGGESTION

n. A suggested quantity or usage, often seen on product packaging. Commonly employed by manufacturers, marketers, and consumers curious about portions.

"Our serving suggestion for the product was 'use as directed,' which said nothing while sounding official."

Related Terms: Cookie-cutter approach, Fluff, Meat and potatoes

SHIT SANDWICH

n. Delivering bad news sandwiched between two positive comments. Commonly employed by managers, HR, and team leads trying to soften criticism.

"The manager's shit sandwich started with a compliment, slammed our performance, then ended with a cheery 'Keep it up!'"

Related Terms: Malicious obedience, CYA (Cover Your Ass), Bullshit bingo

SHANGHAIED

v. Being coerced or tricked into doing something undesirable. Commonly employed informally by employees or colleagues noting forced tasks.

"I was shanghaied into leading the meeting after everyone else vanished behind conveniently closed doors."

Related Terms: Hostage mentality, Playing politics, Micromanagement

SHEEP DIP

n. Mandatory, often tedious corporate briefings applied uniformly to all employees. Commonly employed humorously by staff and critics of forced training.

"The compliance training was a sheep dip: everyone got dunked in the same boring content at once."

Related Terms: Busy work, Management speak, Mushroom principle

SHEEP IT

v. Following a ridiculous company policy without questioning it. Commonly employed ironically by employees acknowledging blind compliance.

"We decided to just sheep it, nodding at every absurd directive to keep the bosses happy."

Related Terms: Mushroom principle, Malicious obedience, Culture fit

SHELFWARE

n. Software purchased but never used, gathering metaphorical dust. Commonly employed by IT, procurement, and cost-conscious managers.

"Our expensive CRM turned into shelfware after we realized spreadsheets were easier and cheaper."

Related Terms: Outdated technology, Cost-benefit analysis, MVP (Minimum Viable Product)

SHIELD TIME

n. Unproductive time spent commuting or behind a windshield. Commonly employed humorously by employees and managers noting travel overhead.

"My shield time tripled when they moved the office to the other side of the galaxy, or so it felt."

Related Terms: Busy work, Donkey work, Hostage mentality

SHIFTING THE BLAME

v. Assigning responsibility for failures to others instead of accepting it. Commonly employed by dysfunctional teams, managers, and colleagues passing the buck.

"Shifting the blame became our office sport, each player dodging accountability like hot potatoes."

Related Terms: CYA (Cover Your Ass), Lack of accountability, Playing politics

SHINY OBJECT SYNDROME

n. Being easily distracted by new trends or ideas, abandoning existing projects prematurely. Commonly employed by managers, analysts, and team members noting lack of focus.

"Our shiny object syndrome led us to chase new tech fads while our core product languished in neglect."

Related Terms: Bubble mentality, Overpromise, underdeliver, Groundhog Day

SHINY OBJECTS

n. Attractive but distracting trends or ideas diverting attention from core goals. Commonly employed by employees, managers, and advisors cautioning against fads.

"We collected shiny objects like magpies, then wondered why real achievements eluded us."

Related Terms: Low-hanging fruit, Cookie-cutter approach, Flesh out

SHIRT SIZE

n. Estimating effort size with categories like small, medium, large. Commonly employed by agile teams, PMs, and developers simplifying complexity estimation.

"We assigned a 'shirt size' to each task: small, medium, large, or 'gargantuan shirt that doesn't exist.'"

Related Terms: A/B testing, Lean methodology, Scope

SHIT EATING GRIN

(Noun) A smug, self-satisfied smile worn by someone who thinks they've outsmarted everyone else, even if they're the only one amused.

Commonly employed by managers, sales reps, and whoever just dodged blame for a failed launch.

"He flashed a shit eating grin as he explained how 'Not my fault' was a valid project status."

Related Terms: Yes-man, Stepford Worker, Overhyped office speak

SHIT SANDWICH

(Noun) Delivering bad news sandwiched between two layers of praise, hoping no one notices the stench in the middle.

Commonly employed by HR, team leads, and managers attempting 'constructive feedback.'

"Our performance review was a shit sandwich: 'Great smile!' ... 'You ruined Q4' ... 'Love your tie!'"

Related Terms: Band-aid solution, Consensus building, Low-hanging fruit

SHOOT THE PUPPY

phrase. Taking an unpopular action or making a difficult decision. Commonly employed by managers, leaders, and colleagues using dark humor.

"When the boss said we had to shoot the puppy, we realized he meant canceling our beloved snack budget—brutal."

Related Terms: Panic-driven decisions, Crisis mode, Burning bridges

SHOOT YOURSELF IN THE FOOT

phrase. To harm one's own cause through careless actions. Commonly employed by managers, teammates, and commentators describing self-inflicted setbacks.

"By insulting our biggest client, we effectively shot ourselves in the foot, then asked the client to sign our cast."

Related Terms: Knee-jerk reactions, Overpromise, underdeliver, Dumpster fire

SHOOTING FROM THE HIP

phrase. Making quick, unconsidered decisions without all relevant information. Commonly employed by employees, managers, and critics noting impulsive moves.

"Our strategy session involved shooting from the hip so often we ran out of ammo and common sense."

Related Terms: Knee-jerk reactions, Crisis mode, Overpromise, underdeliver

SHOOTING THE MESSENGER

phrase. Blaming the bearer of bad news instead of addressing the issue itself. Commonly employed by employees, reporters, and analysts noting unfair blame.

"After I reported low sales, they shot the messenger with a glare that could melt office furniture."

Related Terms: Lack of accountability, CYA (Cover Your Ass), Playing politics

SHORT SALE

n. Selling property for less than what is owed, requiring lender approval. Commonly employed by homeowners, real estate agents, and lenders in distressed sales.

"We tried a short sale, which was shorthand for 'We're losing money, smile anyway.'"

Related Terms: Foreclosure, Investment property, Real estate closing

SHOTGUN APPROACH

n. Using a broad, untargeted strategy hoping something will succeed. Commonly employed by marketers, sales teams, and managers avoiding focus.

"Our shotgun approach to marketing fired ads everywhere, hitting more bystanders than actual customers."

Related Terms: Low-hanging fruit, A/B testing, Over-engineering

SHOULDER TAP

n. A casual, informal request made in passing. Commonly employed by colleagues, managers, and team leads assigning quick tasks.

"He gave me a shoulder tap to handle the report, which is code for 'Here's a chore, enjoy.'"

Related Terms: Chime in, Pencil in, Loop in

SHOVELING SMOKE

phrase. Attempting something intangible or nearly impossible to define. Commonly employed by employees and managers describing futile tasks.

"Trying to measure our 'innovative synergy' felt like shoveling smoke—useless and faintly ridiculous."

Related Terms: Flogging a dead horse, Bubble mentality, Drink the Kool-Aid

SHOW COACH

n. A manager who claims leadership skills but doesn't actually lead. Commonly employed ironically by employees critiquing ineffective bosses.

"Our show coach barked motivational phrases yet never solved problems—an Oscar-worthy performance."

Related Terms: Mediocre leadership, Empty suit, HiPPO (Highest-Paid Person's Opinion)

SHOW PONY

n. Someone who looks good superficially but adds little substance. Commonly employed by coworkers and observers mocking flashy but useless team members.

"The consultant was a show pony, all flash and no fix, wowing us with buzzwords instead of answers."

Related Terms: Empty suit, Corporate lingo, Fluff

SHRINK

n. Retail losses due to theft, errors, or inventory mismanagement. Commonly employed by retailers, loss prevention teams, and operations managers.

"Our shrink rate was so high I suspected the products themselves had legs and dreams of freedom."

Related Terms: Overproduction, Lean waste, Donkey work

SIDEBAR

n. A short, separate conversation held alongside a main meeting. Commonly employed by meeting facilitators, team leads, and colleagues stepping aside for quick chats.

"We held a sidebar to question if the main meeting had any purpose beyond hoarding oxygen."

Related Terms: Chime in, Circle back, Break down silos

SIDEWAYS

adj. A metaphor for a failure or setback. Commonly employed by employees, managers, and commentators describing declining situations.

"The project went sideways so spectacularly it drew applause from Murphy's Law."

Related Terms: Dumpster fire, Death spiral, Melt-down

SIGNATURE BASIS

n. Making decisions or approvals solely based on one's name and reputation. Commonly employed by critics of leadership styles lacking data-driven decisions.

"Hired on signature basis, the new VP had no qualifications besides a fancy last name—impressive or depressing?"

Related Terms: HiPPO (Highest-Paid Person's Opinion), Empty suit, Rubber stamp

SILO

n. When departments or teams work in isolation, avoiding shared information. Commonly employed by executives and consultants critiquing poor cross-team communication.

"Our siloed teams guarded info like dragons hoarding gold, hindering every quest for progress."

Related Terms: Silo mentality, Break down silos, Mushroom principle

SILO MENTALITY

n. A mindset where departments avoid sharing information, hindering collaboration. Commonly employed by managers, leaders, and analysts urging more openness.

"Silo mentality turned our office into a maze of locked doors and whispered secrets—less corporate, more spy thriller."

Related Terms: Silo, Bubble mentality, Herding cats

SILVER BULLET

n. A simple solution perfectly resolving a complex problem. Commonly employed by managers, executives, and consultants yearning for easy fixes.

"We searched for a silver bullet and found a cheap silver-plated spoon—no help, but it looked shiny."

Related Terms: Magic bullet, Panacea, A/B testing

SILVER CEILING

n. An invisible barrier limiting advancement for older employees. Commonly employed by diversity advocates, HR, and career coaches noting age bias.

"Hitting the silver ceiling meant our experienced staff was asked to retire their ambitions and learn how to knit corporate scarves."

Related Terms: Glass ceiling, Culture fit, Meritocracy

SIMMER

v. Allowing an idea or decision to sit before acting on it. Commonly employed by strategists, team leads, and individuals favoring reflection.

"We let the proposal simmer, hoping it wouldn't turn into burnt stew of regret."

Related Terms: Marinate, Let it bake, Circle back

SINGLE PANE OF GLASS

n. Managing or monitoring everything from one unified interface. Commonly employed by IT admins, managers, and tool vendors promising simplicity.

"Our single pane of glass claimed to show all data at once, but mostly showed our reflection of confusion."

Related Terms: Cloud computing, Lean methodology, MVP (Minimum Viable Product)

SINGLE-FAMILY RESIDENCE (SFR)

n. A standalone home designed for one family unit. Commonly employed by real estate agents, buyers, and sellers in housing markets.

"Our SFR listing bragged about 'four walls and a roof,' which is basically House 101."

Related Terms: Greenfield site, Brownfield site, Investment property

SIX SIGMA FALLACY

n. The misconception that applying Six Sigma guarantees best outcomes regardless of context. Commonly employed by critics, quality managers, and analysts noting misused methodologies.

"We clung to Six Sigma like a magic wand, ignoring that it just turned our chaos into measured chaos."

Related Terms: Lean methodology, Over-engineering, Cost-benefit analysis

SKILLS ECOSYSTEM

n. The collective set of skills held by team members within an organization. Commonly employed by HR, L&D departments, and strategists planning workforce capabilities.

"Our skills ecosystem boasted experts in everything except finishing projects before midnight."

Related Terms: Aces in their places, Core competencies, Meritocracy

SKILLSET

n. A set of skills and abilities required for a specific role or task. Commonly employed by recruiters, managers, and career coaches.

"My skillset included writing status updates that said nothing but sounded profound."

Related Terms: Core competency, Green (developing skills), SME (Subject Matter Expert)

SKIP MANAGER

n. Your manager's manager, two levels above you in the hierarchy. Commonly employed by HR, org charts, and employees seeking higher-level input.

"Talking to my skip manager felt like yelling up a very tall tree, hoping a wise owl would respond."

Related Terms: HiPPO (Highest-Paid Person's Opinion), Executive decision, Stakeholder engagement

SKIP-LEVEL MEETING

n. When higher-level management meets directly with employees not in their direct line. Commonly employed by executives, HR, and team leads fostering open communication.

"The skip-level meeting allowed us to tell the VP what we really think, and the VP to politely pretend to care."

Related Terms: In the loop, Chime in, Consensus building

SKULL SESSION

n. A brainstorming meeting focused on generating ideas or solutions. Commonly employed by innovators, creatives, and R&D teams.

"Our skull session ended with empty heads and a shared headache—brainstorming at its finest."

Related Terms: Brain dump, Ideate, Deep dive

SKUNKWORKS (OR SKUNK WORKS PROJECT)

n. A secretive group working on unconventional innovation outside normal processes. Commonly employed by R&D labs, pioneering companies, and innovative leaders.

"We launched a skunkworks project so clandestine even the participants weren't sure what they were building."

Related Terms: Innovation, Regulatory sandbox, Lean startup

SLAVE TRADER

n. A derogatory term for aggressive HR or recruiting practices. Commonly employed humorously or critically by employees describing pushy recruiters.

"Our recruiter's methods were so pushy we jokingly called them a slave trader—HR was not amused."

Related Terms: Culture fit, Hostage mentality, Just filling seats

SLEDULE

n. A project schedule that constantly shifts deadlines without completion. Commonly employed humorously by project teams stuck in perpetual rescheduling.

"We followed a sledule that moved targets like a mirage, always promising relief tomorrow."

Related Terms: Scope creep, Marinate (delayed decisions), Groundhog Day

SLIPPERY SLOPE

n. A situation where one action leads to increasingly negative consequences. Commonly employed by managers, policy analysts, and commentators warning of dangerous precedents.

"Approving one minor exception led us down a slippery slope, ending in a landslide of chaos."

Related Terms: Panic-driven decisions, Death spiral, Flogging a dead horse

SMALL CAP

n. A smaller-scale project or entity considered of lower priority or value. Commonly employed by investors, managers, and analysts classifying initiatives.

"Our small cap initiative was so low priority it lived under the rug, next to last quarter's forgotten ideas."

Related Terms: Donkey work, Busy work, Green (Inexperienced staff)

SMART CONTRACTS

n. Self-executing contracts with terms directly written into code on a blockchain. Commonly employed by blockchain developers, crypto enthusiasts, and futurists.

"We touted smart contracts as revolutionary, then spent days explaining why robots wouldn't sue us."

Related Terms: DeFi (Decentralized Finance), Crypto wallet, FinTech (Financial Technology)

SMELL TEST

n. Using common sense to judge if something seems reasonable or suspicious. Commonly employed by managers, analysts, and decision-makers doing quick evaluations.

"The marketing plan failed the smell test, reeking of desperation and stale ideas."

Related Terms: Sense check, Deep dive, Due diligence

SMIRTING

n. Flirting with co-workers during breaks or social events. Commonly employed humorously by employees, HR might frown upon it.

"Office smirting peaked at the holiday party, where awkward banter met mediocre eggnog."

Related Terms: Scuttlebutt, Culture fit, Chime in

SMOKE AND MIRRORS

n. Deceptive practices creating the illusion of success or effectiveness. Commonly employed by observers, critics, and employees noting superficial tactics.

"Our growth numbers were smoke and mirrors—fancy charts hiding the truth that customers vanished."

Related Terms: Bullshit bingo, Corporate lingo, Overpromise, underdeliver

SMOKESCREEN

n. A distraction or misleading tactic obscuring the truth. Commonly employed by managers, PR teams, and critics noting diversionary strategies.

"The 'exciting new logo' was a smokescreen for our product delay, hoping pretty colors would blind everyone."

Related Terms: Drink the Kool-Aid, Management speak, Bubble mentality

SOCIAL CONTRACT

n. A theory that individuals consent to certain restrictions for the benefit of society. Commonly employed by philosophers, policymakers, and civic educators.

"Our office's social contract: we pretend to care about each other's weekends, and in return, we get minimal back-stabbing."

Related Terms: Public policy, Culture fit, Meritocracy

SOCIAL ENTERPRISE

n. An organization using commercial strategies to achieve social or environmental goals. Commonly employed by CSR leaders, philanthropists, and impact investors.

"We called ourselves a social enterprise for helping charities, though mostly we just sold overpriced coffee."

Related Terms: Philanthropy, Impact investing, CSR (Corporate social responsibility)

SOCIAL IMPACT

n. The effect an organization's actions have on the community or environment. Commonly employed by nonprofits, CSR efforts, and philanthropic foundations.

"Our social impact included one donated pencil and a warm tweet—philanthropy at its pinnacle."

Related Terms: Impact report, Philanthropy, CSR (Corporate social responsibility)

SOCIAL JUSTICE

n. Efforts to achieve fairness and equality in society. Commonly employed by activists, nonprofits, and educators.

"We held a social justice workshop that concluded equality is nice, but can we get back to the budget meeting now?"

Related Terms: Policy advocacy, Public interest litigation, Government accountability

SOCIAL MEDIA ADVOCACY

n. Using social media platforms to promote a cause or raise awareness. Commonly employed by nonprofits, activists, and CSR teams mobilizing support.

"Our social media advocacy campaign got five likes—three from employees, two from bots—mission accomplished?"

Related Terms: Influencer marketing, Crowdfunding, Community outreach

SOCIAL RESPONSIBILITY

n. The duty of organizations to act in ways benefiting society and the environment. Commonly employed by CSR teams, stakeholders, and consumers demanding ethical practices.

"Our social responsibility pledge consisted of recycling one soda can and patting ourselves on the back."

Related Terms: CSR (Corporate social responsibility), Philanthropy, Impact investing

SOCIAL SAFETY NET

n. Government programs supporting those in need (e.g., unemployment benefits, food aid). Commonly employed by policymakers, economists, and social workers.

"The social safety net was more like a safety thread, barely supporting anyone's weight."

Related Terms: Public policy, Economic stimulus, Population health

SOCIAL WELFARE PROGRAMS

n. Government-funded assistance providing financial or other support to citizens in need. Commonly employed by policymakers, nonprofits, and economists.

"Our social welfare program helped many, though the paperwork demanded the patience of a monk."

Related Terms: Social safety net, Public policy, Economic stimulus

SOCIALIZE

v. To share or circulate an idea informally to gather feedback before formal presentation. Commonly employed by managers, team leads, and strategists testing waters.

"We 'socialized' the new policy by forcing everyone to read it, respond, and sign a letter of compliance—so friendly."

Related Terms: Chime in, Circle back, Stakeholder engagement

SOFT PEDAL

v. Downplaying progress or success, giving a false impression of mediocrity. Commonly employed by executives, managers, and PR teams modulating expectations.

"We soft pedaled our improvements, acting modest while secretly hoping someone would notice our genius."

Related Terms: Management speak, Fluff, Bullshit bingo

SOLUTIONING

n. The process of creating and implementing solutions to client problems. Commonly employed by consultants, IT teams, and sales engineers.

"Our solutioning session involved more shrugs than insights, but we called it progress anyway."

Related Terms: Deep dive, A/B testing, Lean methodology

SOUNDBITES

n. Short, impactful statements or key points summarized briefly. Commonly employed by PR, spokespeople, and presenters making messages memorable.

"Our CEO's speech was a series of soundbites so generic they could fit on motivational coffee mugs."

Related Terms: Key takeaway, Management speak, Bullshit bingo

SOUP TO NUTS

phrase. Covering a process from start to finish comprehensively. Commonly employed by consultants, project managers, and trainers.

"We managed the project soup to nuts, which meant we started confused and ended slightly less confused, but fully exhausted."

Related Terms: Deep dive, Marinate, Consensus building

SPACE

n. A slang term for an industry, field, or market segment. Commonly employed by analysts, investors, and marketers referencing broad areas.

"In the marketing space, we shouted slogans until the echo chamber replied, 'Please stop.'"

Related Terms: Go to market, Market analysis, Disruption

SPEAK TO

v. To address or respond directly to a topic or issue. Commonly employed by managers, leaders, and presenters clarifying their remarks.

"Asked to speak to the budget cuts, the CFO danced around the question like a tap-dancing ostrich."

Related Terms: Circle back, Chime in, POV (Point Of View)

SPEAKER-PHONE VOICE

n. The volume or tone people use when on speakerphone, often louder or more stilted. Commonly employed humorously by coworkers or meeting attendees noting odd voice changes.

"On speaker-phone voice, the manager sounded like a game show host announcing our impending deadlines."

Related Terms: In the loop, Sidebar, Stakeholder engagement

SPEAKS TO

v. Indicates that something exemplifies or reflects a particular quality or idea. Commonly employed by managers, analysts, and writers highlighting underlying meanings.

"Our inability to meet deadlines speaks to our talent for creative procrastination."

Related Terms: Key takeaway, Counterfactual, Impact report

SPECIAL PROJECTS

n. Tasks assigned to executives requiring high-level attention, often vague and open-ended. Commonly employed by execs, boards, and senior managers offloading tricky initiatives.

"Special Projects was code for 'Top-secret assignments that confuse everyone and achieve nothing.'"

Related Terms: Punt, Marinate, Mushroom principle

SPECIAL SAUCE

n. A proprietary element providing competitive advantage or unique value. Commonly employed by marketers, brand leads, and strategists touting differentiation.

"Our special sauce turned out to be a blend of guesswork and accidental successes."

Related Terms: Core competencies, Innovation, A/B testing

SPEND

n. The amount of money disbursed for a specific purpose. Commonly employed by CFOs, marketers, and project managers tracking costs.

"Our ad spend rose so high we expected the CFO to faint, but he just twitched and approved more coffee."

Related Terms: ROI (Return on Investment), Cost-benefit analysis, Burn rate

SPIN YOUR WHEELS

v. Working hard without making meaningful progress. Commonly employed by employees, managers, and observers noting futile effort.

"We spun our wheels so hard, we created friction burns on our project timeline."

Related Terms: Busy work, Flogging a dead horse, Groundhog Day

SPINNING PLATES

n. Managing multiple tasks simultaneously, often chaotically. Commonly employed by project managers, busy workers, and teams overloaded with responsibilities.

"Our project manager spun plates with such flair that when they crashed, it was an artistic finale."

Related Terms: Heads down, Herding cats, Crisis mode

SPITBALL

v. To propose ideas informally, often without much detail or planning. Commonly employed by brainstorming teams, creatives, and casual discussions.

"We spent the afternoon spitballing new features, ending up with a notepad of half-baked dreams."

Related Terms: Brain dump, Ideate, Deep dive

SPOKESWEASEL

n. A PR agent who manages communication, often seen as evasive or manipulative. Commonly employed humorously by employees, media, and critics mocking slick PR talk.

"Our spokesweasel delivered carefully crafted statements that said nothing but sounded important."

Related Terms: Management speak, Corporate lingo, Smoke and mirrors

SQUEEZE THE SPONGE

phrase. Extracting every bit of knowledge or value from a resource or individual. Commonly employed by managers, trainers, and teams maximizing expertise.

"We squeezed the sponge of our intern's creativity until even their doodles looked depressed."

Related Terms: Aces in their places, SME (Subject Matter Expert), Core competencies

STAGNATION

n. Lack of growth or progress due to complacency or resistance to change. Commonly employed by managers, strategists, and employees pointing out inertia.

"Our team embraced stagnation like a cozy blanket, refusing to improve unless forced."

Related Terms: Mediocrity, Resistance to change, Bubble mentality

STAKEHOLDER

n. Individuals or groups with an interest in a project's outcome. Commonly employed by project leads, executives, and PMs identifying key parties.

"Our stakeholders demanded results, we demanded sanity—neither got what they wanted."

Related Terms: Stakeholder engagement, Buy-in, In the loop

STAKEHOLDER ENGAGEMENT

n. Involving stakeholders in shaping decisions or initiatives. Commonly employed by project managers, leaders, and consultants ensuring buy-in.

"Our stakeholder engagement sessions featured nodding heads, polite smiles, and zero actionable advice."

Related Terms: Stakeholders, Consensus building, Socialize

STAKEHOLDER MANAGEMENT

n. Gathering opinions and support from key individuals influencing an initiative. Commonly employed by PMs, leaders, and PR teams maintaining good relationships.

"Stakeholder management was like hosting a dinner where everyone's allergic to everything you serve."

Related Terms: Stakeholder engagement, Buy-in, In the loop

STAKEHOLDERING

v. Seeking approval or support from key individuals or groups. Commonly employed humorously by employees and managers joking about excessive consensus-building.

"We spent weeks stakeholdering, a fancy term for pleading nicely while sweating nervously."

Related Terms: Stakeholder management, Stakeholder engagement, Buy-in

STAKEHOLDERS

n. Individuals or groups interested in or impacted by a project's results. Commonly employed by project managers, executives, and consultants mapping influence.

"Our stakeholders ranged from investors to that random guy who insists we should use Comic Sans."

Related Terms: Stakeholder, Stakeholder engagement, In the loop

STALL NAP

n. Taking a quick nap secretly during work hours (sometimes in a restroom stall). Commonly employed humorously by employees needing clandestine breaks.

"A stall nap became my midday vacation spot where ambitions went to snooze."

Related Terms: Burnout, Busy work, Shield time

STANDING ROOM ONLY

phrase. Misleadingly suggesting high demand or availability when none exists. Commonly employed humorously by employees and managers mocking fake urgency.

"The job listing implied standing room only demand, but we discovered tumbleweeds had RSVP'd instead of candidates."

Related Terms: Smoke and mirrors, Bullshit bingo, Overpromise, underdeliver

STARTER MARRIAGE

n. A short first marriage ending quickly, often seen as a learning experience. Commonly employed metaphorically by employees or entrepreneurs describing short-lived ventures.

"Our new venture was like a starter marriage to bad ideas—short-lived and highly educational in what not to do."

Related Terms: Pivot, Lean startup, MVP (Minimum Viable Product)

STATISTICAL MASSAGE

n. Presenting numbers in a manipulated way to achieve a desired conclusion. Commonly employed by analysts, marketers, and spin doctors tweaking data.

"With statistical massage, we made '1 sale' look like 'a 100% increase from zero!'"

Related Terms: Bullshit bingo, Smoke and mirrors, Overpromise, underdeliver

STATUS QUO BIAS

n. Preferring the current state over change. Commonly employed by managers, employees, and advisors calling out fear of innovation.

"Status quo bias kept us clinging to old processes as if new ideas carried rabies."

Related Terms: Resistance to change, Bubble mentality, Mediocrity

STEALTH PARENTING

n. Secretly doing tasks for children while claiming to relax. Commonly employed humorously by parents and multitaskers.

"Stealth parenting at work meant finishing my coworker's reports while pretending I took a break."

Related Terms: Hostage mentality, Busy work, Clock watcher

STEPFORD WORKER

n. An employee who blindly follows corporate agenda without question. Commonly employed ironically by employees critiquing overly compliant colleagues.

"Our Stepford Worker smiled through every absurd directive, a robot in human form."

Related Terms: Culture fit, Mushroom principle, Malicious obedience

STICK TO YOUR KNITTING

phrase. Focusing on one's core competencies rather than wandering into unfamiliar areas. Commonly employed by managers, advisors, and strategists urging focus.

"Management told us to stick to our knitting while they fumbled with a knitting manual upside-down."

Related Terms: Core competencies, Scope, Aces in their places

STICK-AROUND

n. A meeting scheduled immediately after another, forcing participants to remain. Commonly employed humorously by employees trapped in extended sessions.

"We had a stick-around after the already endless meeting — like dessert, but the flavor was despair."

Related Terms: Meeting hell, Busy work, Groundhog Day

STRAP-ON

v. To try something new without prior experience, often awkwardly. Commonly employed humorously by employees or managers experimenting.

"We decided to strap-on a new CRM system with all the grace of toddlers trying on roller skates."

Related Terms: Marinate, A/B testing, Green

STRATEGIC INCOMPETENCE

n. Pretending to be incapable to avoid responsibility. Commonly employed by employees, colleagues, and observers noting clever avoidance.

"Our coworker feigned strategic incompetence at data entry until someone else did it, earning him the Laziness MVP award."

Related Terms: CYA (Cover Your Ass), Playing politics, Lack of accountability

STRATEGIC PLANNING

n. Making plans that are unnecessary because 'planning' already implies strategy (original note). Commonly employed by executives, consultants, and managers emphasizing future direction.

"Our strategic planning meeting debated if we needed another planning meeting — meta inefficiency at its peak."

Related Terms: Roadmap, Deep dive, Consensus building

STRAWMAN

n. A rough version of a proposal intended as a starting point for discussion. Commonly employed by project leads, consultants, and strategists gathering feedback.

"We built a strawman so flimsy that a light breeze of logic knocked it over in seconds."

Related Terms: A/B testing, Marinate, Brain dump

STRESS PUPPY

n. A person constantly anxious or stressed out. Commonly employed humorously by coworkers noting someone's frazzled demeanor.

"We called Jenna a stress puppy—she panicked when the coffee filters ran low, as if civilization ended there."

Related Terms: Burnout, Clock watcher, Mediocrity

STRETCH ASSIGNMENT

n. A task pushing someone beyond their comfort zone to develop new skills. Commonly employed by managers, HR, and team leads encouraging growth.

"My stretch assignment felt like asking a fish to climb a tree and then smile about it."

Related Terms: Aces in their places, Skillset, Meritocracy

SUBSIDIZED HOUSING

n. Housing supported financially by the government to increase affordability. Commonly employed by policymakers, housing authorities, and social workers.

"They offered subsidized housing in a neighborhood so remote that coyotes considered it prime real estate."

Related Terms: Public policy, Social safety net, Community outreach

SUNK COST FALLACY

n. Continuing a failing endeavor due to already invested resources. Commonly employed by analysts, managers, and economists cautioning against bad persistence.

"We sunk so many hours into the project that we refused to quit, even as it sank like a lead submarine."

Related Terms: Scope creep, Perfection paralysis, Cost-benefit analysis

SUNSET

v. Phasing out a product or service over time. Commonly employed by product managers, execs, and IT departments retiring outdated offerings.

"We decided to sunset our old app, watching it set behind the horizon of user complaints."

Related Terms: Digital transformation, Broken workflow, Greenfield site (start anew)

SUNSHINE ENEMA

n. A PR campaign aiming to improve image after bad news, often overly positive. Commonly employed sarcastically by employees, media, and critics mocking forced optimism.

"Our sunshine enema after layoffs included balloons and cheerful emails, fooling no one."

Related Terms: Spin your wheels, Management speak, Smoke and mirrors

SUPER

n. Short for "supervisor." Commonly employed informally by employees and teams referencing direct managers.

"Our super reminded us daily that if we didn't meet targets, neither did their patience."

Related Terms: Helicopter manager, Macromanager, CYA (Cover Your Ass)

SUPPLY-SIDE PLATFORM (SSP)

n. A platform for publishers to sell ad inventory to advertisers programmatically. Commonly employed by publishers, ad sellers, and digital marketing firms.

"Our SSP tried connecting us to eager advertisers, but mostly we got banners for questionable diet pills."

Related Terms: Programmatic advertising, RTB (Real-Time Bidding), Conversion rate

SURFACE

v. To bring attention to a particular issue or topic. Commonly employed by managers, team leads, and reporters highlighting hidden problems.

"We surfaced the budget shortfall, and the CFO thanked me by promoting me to Chief 'Stop Ruining My Day' Officer."

Related Terms: Deep dive, Circle back, Flag

SURPLUSED

adj. A euphemism for being laid off or terminated. Commonly employed by HR, managers, and companies avoiding the word "fired."

"He got surplused, which HR said was corporate slang for 'Fired with a dictionary.'"

Related Terms: CYA (Cover Your Ass), Hostage mentality, Burning bridges

SUSTAINABILITY

n. The ability to maintain and grow operations over time without depleting resources. Commonly employed by CSR teams, nonprofits, and eco-conscious firms.

"Our sustainability plan involved using fewer buzzwords, but we ran out of non-buzzy alternatives."

Related Terms: Value-based care, Client-centric, Green building

SUSTAINABILITY INITIATIVES

n. Government or corporate programs focusing on environmental and social balance. Commonly employed by policymakers, CSR departments, and NGOs.

"Our sustainability initiatives included printing fewer memos and calling it a green revolution."

Related Terms: CSR (Corporate social responsibility), Philanthropy, Impact report

SUSTAINABILITY REPORTING

n. Documenting a company's environmental, social, and governance impacts. Commonly employed by CSR teams, investors, and regulators promoting transparency.

"Our sustainability report read like a bedtime story—lots of good intentions that put everyone to sleep."

Related Terms: Impact report, Philanthropy, Social responsibility

SWAMPLAND IN FLORIDA/ARIZONA

n. A sarcastic remark about unrealistic proposals or deals. Commonly employed informally by employees, critics, and commentators. *"When the vendor promised miracles, we asked if they'd also sell us swampland in Florida."*

Related Terms: Pie in the sky, Magic bullet, Panacea

SWEAT EQUITY

n. Value created by hard work rather than financial investment. Commonly employed by founders, entrepreneurs, and collaborators building from effort.

"We poured sweat equity into the project until we glistened with exhaustion and minimal returns."

Related Terms: [Bootstrapping (not defined; use Lean startup)], Burn rate, Core competencies

SWEAT THE ASSET

v. Maximizing the potential of already overworked employees or resources. Commonly employed by managers, executives, and cost-cutters pressing for more output.

"Management wanted to sweat the asset (us), leaving us feeling like wrung-out sponges."

Related Terms: Risk management, Busy work, Burnout

SWEEPING IT UNDER THE RUG

phrase. Hiding problems or mistakes instead of addressing them openly. Commonly employed by employees, critics, and observers noting denial.

"We swept the data breach under the rug so thoroughly, the rug started looking suspiciously lumpy."

Related Terms: CYA (Cover Your Ass), Playing politics, Overpromise, under-deliver

SWEETHEART DEAL

n. A deal providing highly favorable terms to certain stakeholders, often unfairly. Commonly employed by critics, investors, and analysts calling out preferential treatment.

"Our competitor got a sweetheart deal, leaving us with the sour candy nobody wanted."

Related Terms: Lobbying, Regulatory capture, Public policy

SWIM LANE

n. A visual element in flowcharts or process maps separating responsibilities. Commonly employed by project managers, process designers, and ops teams.

"We drew a swim lane diagram so everyone knew exactly whose lane to blame when things fail."

Related Terms: Break down silos, Matrix team, Critical path

SYMPVERTIZING

n. Using emotional appeal in advertising to create sympathy and connection. Commonly employed by marketers, advertisers, and CSR campaigns.

"Our sympvertizing campaign showed sad puppies to sell software updates—cheap but effective."

Related Terms: Contextual targeting, Bullshit bingo, Retargeting

SYNDICATE

v. To distribute information widely or form a group of investors for a deal. Commonly employed by media outlets, investors, and financial groups.

"We syndicated our newsletter so broadly that even disinterested monks got a copy."

Related Terms: Crowdfunding, Real estate syndication, Programmatic funding

SYNERGY

n. The increased effectiveness resulting from combined efforts. Commonly employed by executives, managers, and consultants hyping collaboration.

"We chanted 'synergy' until it lost meaning and just sounded like a weird sneeze."

Related Terms: Consensus building, Break down silos, Mushroom principle

SYNTHESIZE

v. Combining different pieces of information to form a coherent whole. Commonly employed by analysts, researchers, and team leads summarizing findings.

"After hours of meetings, we synthesized our findings into one sentence: 'We're still confused.'"

Related Terms: Deep dive, Case study, Key takeaway

T
IS FOR TRANSPARENCY BECAUSE TELLING TRUTHS AND TRACKING TRANSACTIONS TRANSFORMS TRUST—TRY TOTAL TRANSPARENCY!

TLA (THREE LETTER ACRONYM)

abbr. + n. Any acronym consisting of three letters, often abundant in business jargon. Commonly employed by corporate teams, technical groups, and consultants using shorthand.

"*We threw around so many TLAs that we needed a separate TLA just to decode them.*"

Related Terms: Management speak, Bullshit bingo, Corporate lingo

TTB (TIME TO BOXES)

abbr. + n. Elapsed meeting time before someone speaks; an inside joke in some workplaces. Commonly employed humorously by employees noting delayed participation.

"*Our TTB hit ten minutes, a record silence broken only by someone coughing politely.*"

Related Terms: Meeting fill, Groundhog Day, Silo mentality

TABLE (SOMETHING)

v. To postpone discussion of a topic until later. Commonly employed by meeting facilitators, team leads, and committees deferring issues.

"*We tabled the budget issue so often the table broke under the weight of ignored topics.*"

Related Terms: Circle back, Marinate, Flesh out

TABLE STAKES

n. The basic requirements or minimum standards needed to be competitive. Commonly employed by strategists, product managers, and market analysts.

"Having a working product is table stakes—so we're already behind since ours crashes on launch."

Related Terms: Core competencies, Low-hanging fruit, A/B testing

TAKE THIS OFFLINE

phrase. To follow up on a topic after the current meeting, usually in private or a smaller group. Commonly employed by managers, facilitators, and team leads controlling meeting scope.

"'Let's take this offline' meant 'I don't want witnesses to the argument we're about to have.'"

Related Terms: Circle back, Sidebar, Break down silos

TAKE TO THE NEXT LEVEL

phrase. To improve something beyond its current standard. Commonly employed by managers, coaches, and motivational speakers pushing further improvement.

"We took the strategy to the next level, which was basically the same level with a nicer PowerPoint template."

Related Terms: Iterate, Growth hacking, A/B testing

TAKING CREDIT

v. Claiming success or achievements made by others as one's own. Commonly employed by critics, team members, and managers calling out unfair glory.

"Our boss mastered taking credit: when the team succeeded, it was his vision; when we failed, it was our folly."

Related Terms: CYA (Cover Your Ass), Shifting the blame, Playing politics

TALKING HEADS

n. People who speak a lot in meetings without adding real value or action items. Commonly employed by meeting attendees, critics, and observers of empty discussions.

"The meeting was full of talking heads, blabbing like TV pundits on a slow news day."

Related Terms: Bullshit bingo, Management speak, Meanderthal

TANGENTERY

n. Discussions or topics straying away from the main subject. Commonly employed humorously by colleagues noting off-topic rambles.

"Our meeting devolved into tangentery, debating donut flavors instead of project deadlines."

Related Terms: In the weeds, Broken record, Groundhog Day

TAP DANCER

n. Someone appearing busy and productive without achieving meaningful results.- Commonly employed by coworkers and managers mocking superficial hustle.

"Our tap dancer shuffled papers and nodded a lot, accomplishing about as much as a broken clock."

Related Terms: Show pony, Empty suit, Management speak

TART UP

v. To make something appear more attractive or appealing, often superficially. Commonly employed by marketers, product teams, and presenters adding cosmetic improvements.

"We tarted up the old product with new colors and called it Version 2.0—ta-da!"

Related Terms: Cookie-cutter approach, Fluff, Marketecture

TASKED

v. Assigned a specific task or responsibility. Commonly employed by managers, leaders, and project leads delegating work.

"I was tasked with creating yet another report no one would read—thrilling."

Related Terms: Deliverables, SOW (Scope Of Work), Skillset

TASSEL-LOAFERS

n. Visitors who stand out in a construction site due to their formal or stylish shoes. Commonly employed humorously by workers mocking overdressed executives touring facilities.

"The tassel-loafers toured our grimy factory floor, looking as out of place as opera singers in a punk concert."

Related Terms: Management speak, Culture fit, Bullshit bingo

TAX-EXEMPT STATUS

n. A designation allowing an organization to avoid certain taxes due to its nature or purpose. Commonly employed by nonprofits, religious institutions, and educational organizations.

"Our nonprofit's tax-exempt status made us feel like financial Houdinis, escaping the clutches of the IRS."

Related Terms: 501(c)(3), Philanthropy, Nonprofit compliance

TEAM KILLER

n. An individual whose behavior undermines team effectiveness. Commonly employed by managers and coworkers identifying toxic influences.

"The team killer appeared cheerful, yet somehow triggered infighting with a single raised eyebrow."

Related Terms: Toxic culture, Burning bridges, Playing politics

TECH ECOSYSTEM

n. The network of companies, technologies, and individuals supporting a specific tech sector. Commonly employed by investors, analysts, and entrepreneurs describing industry structures.

"In our tech ecosystem, startups and investors danced a tango of buzzwords and questionable valuations."

Related Terms: Innovation, Disruption, Digital transformation

TECH STACK

n. The collection of technologies, programming languages, and tools used by a company. Commonly employed by developers, IT teams, and product managers.

"Our tech stack resembled a junk drawer of tools we barely understood, all duct-taped together with hope."

Related Terms: Over-engineering, Technical debt, Cloud computing

TECHNICAL DEBT

n. The accumulated cost of maintaining outdated, inefficient, or poorly written code. Commonly employed by developers, engineers, and CTOs acknowledging long-term code issues.

"Our technical debt grew so large we considered charging it rent—at least then it would pay for its mess."

Related Terms: Over-engineering, Lean methodology, Iterate

TEE UP

v. Preparing or organizing something in advance so it's ready for use. Commonly employed by managers, admins, and leaders ensuring smooth starts.

"We teed up the presentation, which meant loading slides and praying the audience didn't ask questions."

Related Terms: Marinate, Circle back, Cadence

TEFLON SHOULDERS

n. Someone adept at avoiding blame or responsibility, letting issues slide off. Commonly employed humorously by employees, managers, or coworkers.

"With Teflon shoulders, the manager let every mistake slide off, as if error-proofing came standard."

Related Terms: CYA (Cover Your Ass), Shifting the blame, Lack of accountability

TELEHEALTH

n. Providing healthcare services remotely via telecommunications. Commonly employed by hospitals, clinics, and insurers offering virtual visits.

"Telehealth allowed patients to get medical advice from their sofa, but didn't prevent doctors from diagnosing 'bad Wi-Fi.'"

Related Terms: Telemedicine, Care coordination, Value-based care

TELEMEDICINE

n. Remote clinical services provided via technology, like video consultations. Commonly employed by hospitals, clinics, and insurers expanding care access.

"Our telemedicine calls combined medical expertise with pixelated faces and well-timed audio lags."

Related Terms: Telehealth, Chronic care management, EHR (Electronic Health Record)

TENANT IMPROVEMENT

n. Modifications made to a rental property to meet a tenant's needs. Commonly employed by landlords, property managers, and commercial tenants.

"Our tenant improvements included removing the shag carpet from the '70s and adding lights that didn't flicker ominously."

Related Terms: Build-to-suit, Property management, Lease agreement

TENANT SCREENING

n. Evaluating prospective tenants through rental history, credit scores, etc. Commonly employed by landlords, property managers, and screening services.

"After tenant screening, we learned our applicant once tried to pay rent in Monopoly money—pass."

Related Terms: Property management, Real estate closing, Greenfield site

TESTICULATE

v. To gesture wildly while talking, often without substantial content. Commonly employed humorously by coworkers mocking dramatic but empty speeches.

"Our VP testiculated during the pitch, waving arms like a windmill of nonsense."

Related Terms: Meanderthal, Bullshit bingo, Management speak

THAT DOG WON'T HUNT

phrase. An idea or plan that won't succeed or isn't workable. Commonly employed by managers, coworkers, and critics dismissing proposals.

"After hours of debate, we concluded that our pricing strategy was so flawed that dog won't hunt."

Related Terms: Knee-jerk reactions, Broken record, Pie in the sky

THE JUICE IS NOT WORTH THE SQUEEZE

phrase. The effort or cost isn't justified by the outcome. Commonly employed by employees, managers, and friends warning against low ROI.

"We poured hours into the project only to realize the juice wasn't worth the squeeze—we tasted regret."

Related Terms: Cost-benefit analysis, Sunk cost fallacy, Overpromise, under-deliver

THINK OUTSIDE THE BOX

phrase. Encouraging creative, unconventional thinking. Commonly employed by managers, mentors, and motivational speakers.

"Our attempt to think outside the box led us into a labyrinth of bizarre ideas and no exit signs."

Related Terms: Deep dive, Ideate, Brain dump

THINK THE UNTHINKABLE

phrase. Considering possibilities normally deemed too extreme or unrealistic. Commonly employed by innovators, strategists, and crisis planners.

"We tried to think the unthinkable and ended up imagining a world where our product launched on time—truly radical."

Related Terms: Counterfactual, Disruption, Innovation

THIRD-PARTY DATA

n. Data collected by an external company, not directly from the user. Commonly employed by advertisers, marketers, and analysts broadening data sources.

"Relying on third-party data meant trusting a stranger's notes on our customers, who might just be bored cats on the internet."

Related Terms: Programmatic advertising, Cookie tracking, Conversion rate

THOUGHT LEADER

n. An individual widely recognized as an authority in a particular field. Commonly employed by marketers, PR teams, and personal branding experts.

"Our CEO wants to be seen as a thought leader—time to post more LinkedIn articles about 'disruption.'"

Related Terms: Influencer marketing, Innovation, Mushroom principle

THOUGHT SHOWER

n. A brainstorming session aiming to generate new ideas. Commonly employed by teams, facilitators, and creative workshops.

"We had a thought shower that felt more like a thought drizzle—just damp enough to be irritating."

Related Terms: Brain dump, Ideate, Deep dive

THREE-MARTINI LUNCH

n. A business lunch involving multiple alcoholic beverages, considered outdated or indulgent. Commonly employed humorously by employees and managers referencing old-school corporate culture.

"We joked about a three-martini lunch, but with our deadlines, even a three-coffee lunch felt risky."

Related Terms: Travel dazzle, Bullshit bingo, Donkey work

THROW THE DOLLY OUT OF THE PRAM

phrase. Having a tantrum or emotional outburst. Commonly employed humorously by coworkers and managers noting childish reactions.

"When the client rejected our proposal, the PM threw the dolly out of the pram, stomping off Slack dramatically."

Related Terms: Throwing a tantrum, Broken record, Mushroom principle

THROW UNDER THE BUS

phrase. To blame or sacrifice someone else for self-protection or gain. Commonly employed by employees, managers, and observers noting scapegoating.

"We threw the intern under the bus so often that we named a bus route after them."

Related Terms: Shifting the blame, CYA (Cover Your Ass), Playing politics

THROWING A TANTRUM

phrase. Reacting with exaggerated frustration or anger over minor issues. Commonly employed by colleagues, managers, and observers describing unprofessional behavior.

"Our designer threw a tantrum when asked to change the font size, as if we asked for Papyrus."

Related Terms: Flogging a dead horse, Herding cats (chaotic environment), Malicious obedience

THROWING SOMEONE UNDER THE BUS

phrase. Another form of 'throw under the bus,' sacrificing someone else to avoid blame. Commonly employed by employees, teams, and commentators noting scapegoating.

"When asked who missed the deadline, we all pointed to Dave, collectively pushing him under that metaphorical bus."

Related Terms: Throw under the bus, Shifting the blame, CYA (Cover Your Ass)

TIGER TEAM

n. A small group of experts tackling a specific, urgent challenge. Commonly employed by crisis managers, security teams, and innovation squads.

"We formed a tiger team to fix the product's security flaw before hackers pounced."

Related Terms: S.W.A.T. team, Crisis management, Risk management

TIME PIG

n. A project consuming excessive time and resources with little result. Commonly employed by teams and managers frustrated with resource drains.

"Our marketing campaign was a time pig, devouring hours and producing oinks of disappointment."

Related Terms: Busy work, Burn rate, Sunk cost fallacy

TIME-POOR

adj. Having too little time to engage in personal or non-work activities. Commonly employed by busy professionals, managers, and employees lamenting overload.

"We were so time-poor that scheduling a coffee break felt like planning a secret heist."

Related Terms: Burnout, Shield time, Busy work

TIMEBOX

v. To allocate a fixed amount of time for a task to improve efficiency and focus. Commonly employed by agile teams, project managers, and productivity coaches.

"We'll timebox this brainstorm to 15 minutes—after that, no more arguing about button colors."

Related Terms: Lean methodology, A/B testing, Scope

TIMEFRAME

n. A set or approximate period in which a task or project must be completed. Commonly employed by PMs, managers, and clients setting deadlines.

"Our timeframe stretched like taffy, sweet but never quite solidifying into a deadline."

Related Terms: Marinate, Circle back, Cadence

TIPS AND PEARLS

n. Short pieces of advice or small insights, often shared informally. Commonly employed by mentors, colleagues, and trainers offering quick guidance.

"Our tips and pearls included 'Don't anger the CFO' and 'Always check if the microphone is off.'"

Related Terms: Key takeaway, Learnings, Flesh out

TITLE INSURANCE

n. Insurance protecting buyers and lenders against defects in a property's title. Commonly employed by homebuyers, lenders, and real estate attorneys.

"We bought title insurance just in case the property's previous owner was a ghostly claimant."

Related Terms: Real estate closing, Investment property, Escrow

TITLE SPONSOR

n. A company that provides financial support and gets naming rights. Commonly employed by event organizers, nonprofits, and marketers seeking branding prominence. "

Our title sponsor insisted we rename the conference room 'The Synergy Suite of Awesomeness.'"

Related Terms: Corporate sponsorship, CSR (Corporate social responsibility), Philanthropy

TO YOUR POINT

phrase. Acknowledging a previous comment while connecting to a new topic or idea. Commonly employed by facilitators, colleagues, and managers building on discussions.

"To your point about 'efficiency,' yes, we are indeed consistently breaking speed records in confusion."

Related Terms: Chime in, Circle back, POV (Point Of View)

TOKEN EFFORT

n. A minimal or superficial attempt to appear as though trying. Commonly employed by coworkers, managers, and critics noting insincere attempts.

"Our token effort to fix user complaints was changing the button color—truly groundbreaking improvement."

Related Terms: Busy work, Overpromise, underdeliver, Fluff

TOKENISM

n. Including minorities or underrepresented groups superficially for appearance's sake. Commonly employed by diversity advocates, HR, and critics of shallow inclusion.

"Our diversity initiative amounted to tokenism: one intern from a different background and a self-congratulatory email."

Related Terms: Culture fit, Glass ceiling, Elitism

TOKENIZATION

n. Converting assets or rights into digital tokens on a blockchain. Commonly employed by blockchain developers, fintech innovators, and crypto enthusiasts.

"We tokenized our customer rewards program so even our confusion was now stored on a blockchain."

Related Terms: Smart contracts, DeFi (Decentralized Finance), FinTech (Financial Technology)

TOKENOMICS

n. The economic design behind cryptocurrencies or tokens, including issuance and distribution. Commonly employed by crypto investors, blockchain startups, and DeFi analysts.

"Our tokenomics plan read like a sci-fi novel: exciting buzzwords, unclear plot, and questionable reality."

Related Terms: Tokenization, DeFi (Decentralized Finance), FinTech (Financial Technology)

TONY BAGADONUTS

n. A humorous, informal term for a clumsy or bumbling person. Commonly employed jokingly by colleagues or friends mocking harmless incompetence.

"After tripping over the cable and spilling coffee, Gary earned the nickname Tony Bagadonuts."

Related Terms: Scrub, Donkey work, Mushroom principle (all quirky references)

TOO MANY COOKS IN THE KITCHEN

phrase. When too many people are involved, causing inefficiency and confusion. Commonly employed by managers, team leads, and participants in overcrowded projects.

"We had so many stakeholders that deciding on font size was like a UN summit on typography."

Related Terms: Groundhog Day, Silo mentality, Consensus building

TOOLKIT

n. A set of tools or resources designed for a specific purpose. Commonly employed by trainers, educators, and consultants offering support materials.

"Our employee toolkit included a pen, a manual, and a headache—useful."

Related Terms: Capacity building, Core competencies, Learnings

TOP OF MIND

phrase. A top priority or key focus of attention. Commonly employed by managers, leaders, and communicators highlighting main concerns.

"Staying profitable was top of mind, second only to finding more coffee."

Related Terms: Cadence, Key takeaway, Go-to-market strategy

TOUCH BASE

v. Briefly contacting someone to discuss updates or check progress. Commonly employed by managers, colleagues, and clients keeping communication open.

"'Let's touch base' meant scheduling another meeting to say we have nothing new to share."

Related Terms: Chime in, Loop in, Circle back

TOUCHPOINT

n. Any interaction between a business and its customers. Commonly employed by marketers, CX teams, and product managers mapping user journeys.

"Every customer touchpoint reminded us that customers prefer fewer touchpoints and more actual service."

Related Terms: Customer journey, Conversion rate, A/B testing

TOWN HALL

n. A company-wide meeting led by senior management discussing important issues. Commonly employed by executives, HR, and leaders promoting transparency.

"Our town hall promised transparency and delivered slides so vague we thought we were reading hieroglyphs."

Related Terms: Consensus building, Stakeholder engagement, Chime in

TOXIC CULTURE

n. A workplace environment marked by negativity, unethical behavior, or poor leadership. Commonly employed by employees, HR, and consultants addressing dysfunction.

"Our office's toxic culture meant smiling was suspicious and asking for help was a sign of weakness."

Related Terms: Team killer, Playing politics, Mediocrity

TRACTION

n. Measurable progress or momentum toward a goal. Commonly employed by startups, product teams, and investors seeking validation.

"We bragged about traction until someone asked for numbers, and we stalled like a car without gas."

Related Terms: A/B testing, Growth hacking, Product-market fit

TRANSITIONING

n. Undergoing a significant change or shift, often clumsily. Commonly employed by managers, team leads, and employees adapting to new systems.

"We were transitioning to a new system, which meant we hovered in a state of perpetual half-brokenness."

Related Terms: Change management, Marinate, Iterate

TRANSPARENCY

n. Openness, clarity, and visibility in actions, decisions, and information sharing. Commonly employed by leaders, auditors, and stakeholders demanding honesty.

"Our leadership promised transparency, then released a report so redacted it resembled abstract art."

Related Terms: Governmental transparency, Regulatory compliance, Chatham House Rules

TRANSPARENCY ACT

n. Legislation aimed at ensuring openness in government spending or activities. Commonly employed by policymakers, watchdogs, and citizens seeking accountability.

"Under the Transparency Act, we learned the government spent $10K on mystery consultants named 'N/A.'"

Related Terms: Government accountability, Public policy, FOIA (Freedom of information act)

TRANSPARENCY INTERNATIONAL

n. A global organization fighting corruption and promoting openness in government. Commonly employed by activists, policymakers, and journalists.

"Transparency International would weep if they saw our accounting methods—so would our accountants." Related Terms: Government accountability, Public policy, Policy advocacy

TRAVEL DAZZLE

n. Showy attempts to impress a superior during business trips. Commonly employed humorously by employees mocking forced corporate tourism. *"Our travel dazzle included insisting on fancy dinners and Uber rides to the cafe next door."*

Related Terms: Three-martini lunch, Bullshit bingo, Corporate lingo

TREE KILLER

n. Someone who prints every document unnecessarily, killing trees. Commonly employed humorously by coworkers noting wasteful printing habits. *"Bob printed his emails, his calendar, and his reminders to print less, earning the title 'Tree Killer.'"*

Related Terms: Busy work, Fluff, Mushroom principle

TREEWARE

n. Printed materials, as opposed to digital versions. Commonly employed by eco-conscious employees or archivists joking about paper docs. *"Our proposal arrived in treeware form, heavy enough to double as office furniture."*

Related Terms: Hard copy, Paper, Cookie-cutter approach

TRENDING OVER

v. Exceeding a projected value or budget. Commonly employed by analysts, managers, and finance teams noting overshoot. *"We trended over budget so consistently that 'under budget' became a mythical phrase we joked about."*

Related Terms: Burn rate, Cost-benefit analysis, Overpromise, underdeliver

TRIAL BALLOON

n. Sharing information or a proposal tentatively to gauge reactions before committing. Commonly employed by managers, policymakers, and leaders testing waters.

"We floated a trial balloon on raising prices—consumers popped it faster than we said 'just kidding.'"

Related Terms: Counterfactual, Marinate, A/B testing

TRIANGULATE

v. Estimating a situation using multiple data points or perspectives. Commonly employed by analysts, researchers, and strategists seeking accuracy.

"We triangulated sales forecasts and discovered we'd be successful if reality took a vacation."

Related Terms: Deep dive, Due diligence, Sense check

TRIBAL KNOWLEDGE

n. Unwritten, collective wisdom passed within an organization over time. Commonly employed by managers, long-time employees, and new hires lacking documentation.

"Our tribal knowledge lived in Carol's head—when she retired, half our processes vanished with her."

Related Terms: Mushroom principle, Institutional memory, Silo mentality

TRIM THE FAT

v. Removing unnecessary elements to improve efficiency. Commonly employed by managers, consultants, and cost-cutters.

"We tried to trim the fat, but ended up cutting muscle and leaving the flab—nice job."

Related Terms: Value engineering, Lean methodology, Over-engineering

TRIPLE-DUB

n. A playful term for the 'www' in a website address. Commonly employed humorously by employees referencing old-school internet.

"We told clients to check triple-dub dot oursite, feeling very 1997 as we said it."

Related Terms: Cloud computing, E-commerce, Cookie-cutter approach (just for contrast)

TRUE NORTH

n. The ideal direction or principle guiding a business toward success. Commonly employed by strategists, leaders, and coaches emphasizing core mission.

"Our true north was profit, but the compass kept pointing to chaos and late-night pizza runs."

Related Terms: Core values, Vision, Business transformation

TRUSTAFARIAN

n. A young co-worker perceived as privileged due to inherited wealth and lacking effort. Commonly employed humorously by colleagues mocking entitled behavior.

"Our trustafarian intern strolled in at noon, calling it an 'early start'—privilege at its finest."

Related Terms: Culture fit, Green (inexperience), Empty suit

TURD POLISHING

n. Attempting to make a bad situation or product appear better than it is. Commonly employed by employees, marketers, and managers humorously acknowledging futility.

"We spent hours turd polishing the failed campaign report, hoping shiny nonsense impressed the boss."

Related Terms: Smoke and mirrors, Bullshit bingo, Overpromise, underdeliver

TURKEY FARM

n. A department where underperforming employees are placed instead of addressing issues. Commonly employed humorously by employees noting organizational avoidance.

"They transferred Bob to the turkey farm—apparently, that's what we call the basement office now."

Related Terms: Mediocrity, Cutthroat (contrast with no improvement), Silo mentality

TURKEY TROT

n. Moving problematic employees around instead of solving underlying problems. Commonly employed humorously by coworkers and managers acknowledging avoidance.

"Our turkey trot rotated troublemakers like musical chairs, never solving why the music was off-key."

Related Terms: Mushroom principle, Malicious obedience, Playing politics

TURN-KEY SOLUTION

phrase. A fully ready product or service needing minimal setup. Commonly employed by vendors, consultants, and IT teams seeking quick deployment.

"They sold us a turn-key solution, but the instructions read like a riddle."

Related Terms: Build-to-suit, Single pane of glass, MVP (Minimum Viable Product)

TWO CENTS

n. Offering one's opinion or suggestion informally. Commonly employed by colleagues, managers, and friends adding a quick thought.

"My two cents on the matter: we're doomed—but in a charming, learn-as-we-go way."

Related Terms: Chime in, Brain dump, Marinate

TWO-COMMA

adj. Referring to anything costing over $1 million (which has two commas in the number). Commonly employed by investors, execs, and insiders bragging about large sums.

"Our two-comma deal sounded impressive until we realized we spent more on lawyers than the product."

Related Terms: VC (Venture Capital), FinTech (Financial Technology), Burn rate

TWOBICLE

n. A cubicle designed for two people, often larger or more spacious. Commonly employed by office managers and facilities teams in shared workspaces.

"We shared a twobicle, which meant enjoying the sweet sound of each other's sighs all day."

Related Terms: Hot desking, Culture fit, Matrix team

U

IS FOR UNICORN BECAUSE UNVEILING A UNICORN ULTIMATELY UNLEASHES UNBELIEVABLE UPSIDES—UPEND MEDIOCRITY!

UI/UX (USER INTERFACE/USER EXPERIENCE)

abbr. + n. UI focuses on visual elements; UX focuses on overall user journey and satisfaction. Commonly employed by designers, developers, and product teams.

"Our UI was pretty, but our UX made customers feel like hamsters in a maze—cute, but trapped."

Related Terms: A/B testing, Customer journey, Conversion rate

UBER

adj. Used as a prefix to mean exceptional or beyond the norm. Commonly employed by marketers, fans, and critics exaggerating greatness.

"Our uber marketing strategy involved shouting louder and adding 'super' before every feature name."

Related Terms: Bullshit bingo, Corporate lingo, Overpromise, underdeliver

UNBUNDLING

v. Breaking a service package into smaller, targeted components. Commonly employed by product teams, strategists, and innovators offering à la carte options.

"We tried unbundling features so customers could buy them separately—an a la carte menu of mild disappointment."

Related Terms: Freemium, Lean methodology, Cookie-cutter approach

UNCLEAR SPECIFICATIONS

n. Poorly defined or constantly changing requirements causing confusion and errors. Commonly employed by developers, PMs, and teams struggling with vague inputs.

"Our unclear specs were like riddles from a mischievous elf—just less fun and more costly."

Related Terms: Broken workflow, Scope creep, Flesh out

UNDER THE RADAR

phrase. Operating quietly or unnoticed, often to avoid scrutiny. Commonly employed by startups, skunkworks teams, and cautious managers.

"We launched the beta under the radar, hoping no one would notice the bugs tap-dancing in the code."

Related Terms: Skunkworks, Regulatory sandbox, Counterfactual

UNDER-UTILIZED ASSETS

n. Equipment or resources not used to their full potential, causing waste. Commonly employed by operations managers, asset managers, and efficiency experts.

"Our office had under-utilized assets: a coffee machine that never worked and a ping-pong table collecting dust."

Related Terms: Lean waste, Capacity constraints, Maintenance backlog

UNDERTOOLED

adj. Lacking the necessary tools, resources, or equipment to work effectively. Commonly employed by employees, managers, and IT teams noting shortages.

"We were undertooled for video editing—our best software was a decade-old trial version."

Related Terms: Maintenance backlog, Scalability issues, Broken workflow

UNDERWATER BASKET WEAVING

n. A term for a useless or impractical activity. Commonly employed humorously by employees mocking pointless tasks.

"Our training felt like underwater basket weaving—difficult and serving no real-world purpose."

Related Terms: Busy work, Donkey work, Flogging a dead horse

UNICORN

n. A privately held startup valued at over $1 billion. Commonly employed by investors, entrepreneurs, and media praising rare successes.

"We dreamed of becoming a unicorn, but struggled to afford a paper horn for the office mascot."

Related Terms: VC (Venture Capital), Disruption, FinTech (Financial Technology)

UNIVERSAL BASIC INCOME (UBI)

n. A government program providing every citizen with a regular, unconditional sum of money. Commonly employed by policymakers, economists, and activists debating social safety nets.

"Under UBI, everyone gets paid for existing, which beats our current pay-for-exhaustion model."

Related Terms: Social safety net, Social welfare programs, Public policy

UNKNOWN UNKNOWN

n. Risks or issues not yet identified or imagined. Commonly employed by risk managers, strategists, and planners acknowledging uncertainty.

"We feared unknown unknowns, the boogeymen lurking behind every Gantt chart."

Related Terms: Counterfactual, Risk management, Crisis mode

UNPACK

v. Analyzing or explaining a topic in more detail. Commonly employed by analysts, presenters, and educators clarifying complexities.

"We tried to unpack the strategy, finding layers of confusion and stale metaphors tucked inside."

Related Terms: Deep dive, Flesh out, Marinate

UNRESTRICTED FUNDS

n. Donations a nonprofit can use for any purpose related to its mission. Commonly employed by nonprofits, foundations, and donors valuing flexibility.

"With unrestricted funds, we finally replaced the leaking roof, instead of just handing out more brochures."

Related Terms: 501(c)(3), Grant funding, Programmatic funding

UNSCREW

v. To fix or reverse damage caused by a poor decision or mistake. Commonly employed humorously by employees and managers correcting errors.

"We tried to unscrew the mess by apologizing, refunding, and offering a free hug—desperation never looked so friendly."

Related Terms: Crisis management, Fixing broken workflow (Broken workflow), Due diligence

UP STICKS

v. Closing down a location or office and relocating elsewhere. Commonly employed by employees, managers, and commentators noting moves.

"We decided to up sticks and move to a new city, guessing sunshine might improve our mood."

Related Terms: Government privatization, Transitioning, Exit strategy

UP THE PITCH

v. Intensifying the level of an argument or discussion. Commonly employed by negotiators, debaters, and team leads applying pressure.

"When negotiations stalled, we upped the pitch to a shrill note of desperation."

Related Terms: Playing politics, Shifting the blame, Knee-jerk reactions

UPFEED

v. Passing key or important information upward in the hierarchy. Commonly employed by employees, managers, and organizations maintaining top-down awareness.

"We tried to upfeed our concerns to management, who promptly downfed us vague reassurances."

Related Terms: In the loop, POC (Point Of Contact), SPOC (Single Point Of Contact)

UPSHOT

n. The final or most important result from a situation. Commonly employed by analysts, managers, and stakeholders summarizing outcomes.

"The upshot of the meeting was we wasted an hour concluding what we knew at the start: nothing changed."

Related Terms: Key takeaway, Deep dive, Consensus building

UPSKILL

v. Improving one's skills or knowledge through training or practice. Commonly employed by HR, L&D, and managers preparing teams for future needs.

"We invested in upskilling our staff, hoping they'd stop staring blankly at the new software."

Related Terms: Skillset, Stretch assignment, Green

UPSPEAK

n. Ending sentences with a rising intonation, making statements sound like questions. Commonly employed by communication coaches, linguists, and managers noting speech habits.

"Our intern's upspeak made even confident facts sound like timid guesses?"

Related Terms: Management speak, Meanderthal, Bullshit bingo

UPTITLING

v. Giving employees more prestigious job titles without changing their role. Commonly employed by HR, managers, and executives trying to boost morale cheaply.

"After uptitling, our receptionist became 'Chief Entrance Experience Officer,' impressing no one."

Related Terms: Empty suit, Show pony, Culture fit

URBAN SPRAWL

n. The uncontrolled expansion of urban areas into surrounding rural land. Commonly employed by urban planners, environmentalists, and policymakers.

"Urban sprawl turned our quiet suburb into a traffic jam with expensive coffee."

Related Terms: Public policy, Regional development, Brownfield site

USER ACQUISITION

n. Gaining new users or customers for a product or service. Commonly employed by marketers, growth hackers, and product teams.

"Our user acquisition strategy was so subtle, we might as well have screamed 'Buy now, you fools!' at passersby."

Related Terms: Conversion rate, A/B testing, Go-to-market strategy

V

IS FOR VALUE PROPOSITION BECAUSE VALIDATING VALUE VISIBLY VANQUISHES VACANT VOWS—VERIFY YOU'RE VITAL, NOT VAPOR!

VF (VERSION FINAL)

abbr. + n. A tag for the final version of a file. Commonly employed by editors, designers, and team leads naming document versions.

"We saved it as vF, confident this was the end, until someone demanded changes and we became vF_final_final."

Related Terms: Paper, Due diligence, Hard copy

VC (VENTURE CAPITAL)

abbr. + n. Financing where investors fund early-stage companies in exchange for equity. Commonly employed by startups, investors, and entrepreneurs.

"The VC listened politely, nodded, and invested elsewhere, leaving us to wonder if we pitched a lemonade stand as a tech unicorn."

Related Terms: Unicorn, FinTech (Financial Technology), Seed round

VR (VIRTUAL REALITY)

abbr. + n. Technology creating fully immersive, computer-generated environments. Commonly employed by product teams, gaming companies, and marketers enhancing experiences.

"In VR, our meeting room looked cooler, but we still accomplished as little as reality allowed."

Related Terms: AR (Augmented Reality), Innovation, Cross-channel marketing

VALUE ADD

n. Enhancements or improvements that increase the worth or appeal of a product or service. Commonly employed by sales teams, marketers, and consultants highlighting benefits.

"We added a talking chatbot as a value add, hoping customers prefer friendly nonsense to silence."

Related Terms: Value proposition, Core competencies, Customer-centric

VALUE CHAIN

n. The series of activities adding value to a product or service from creation to delivery. Commonly employed by strategists, operations managers, and consultants mapping processes.

"Our value chain had many links, most of which rattled ominously and added no actual value."

Related Terms: Lean methodology, Overproduction, Break down silos

VALUE ENGINEERING

n. Reducing costs while preserving as much quality as possible. Commonly employed by manufacturers, engineers, and procurement teams cutting expenses.

"After value engineering, our product went from a 'deluxe car' to 'a bicycle with stickers,' but hey, it's cheaper now."

Related Terms: Trim the fat, Cost-benefit analysis, Lean waste

VALUE PROP / VALUE PROPOSITION

n. A statement explaining why a product or service is beneficial and worth choosing. Commonly employed by marketers, sales teams, and product managers.

"Our value proposition boiled down to 'Buy this, maybe you won't regret it'—a pitch for the ages."

Related Terms: Core competency, Customer journey, A/B testing

VALUE PROPOSITION

n. The unique value a product or service offers, persuading customers to choose it over alternatives. Commonly employed by branding teams, marketers, and strategists.

"We repeated the value proposition until it lost meaning, kind of like saying 'innovate' 100 times fast."

Related Terms: Value add, User acquisition, Conversion rate

VALUE-BASED CARE

n. A healthcare model rewarding providers for patient health outcomes rather than service volume. Commonly employed by insurers, healthcare systems, and policymakers. "

Value-based care meant we couldn't bill for every band-aid, forcing us to consider actual healing."

Related Terms: Care coordination, Capitation, Bundled payments

VERBIAGE

n. Excessive or unnecessary words used to explain something. Commonly employed by editors, writers, and critics of bloated documents.

"Our report's verbiage resembled a dictionary explosion — long-winded and zero clarity."

Related Terms: Fluff, Management speak, Corporate lingo

VERBIFICATION

n. Turning a noun into a verb, often in modern business jargon. Commonly employed humorously by employees mocking language trends.

"We verbified 'action' into 'actioning,' because why speak plainly when you can complicate language?"

Related Terms: Verbing, Bullshit bingo, Corporate lingo

VERBING

n. Using a noun as a verb to imply action, common in tech or business talk. Commonly employed by writers, communicators, and critics of jargon.

"We started verbing everything — 'Let's calendar that' — until normal English fled our meetings."

Related Terms: Verbification, Management speak, Bullshit bingo

VERTICAL

n. A specific market or industry segment. Commonly employed by sales teams, marketers, and strategists focusing on niches.

"We focused on the healthcare vertical, ignoring that our product was a stapler unrelated to health or care."

Related Terms: Market analysis, Go-to-market strategy, Value proposition

VICIOUS AGREEMENT

n. When everyone enthusiastically agrees but no actual decision or action occurs.

Commonly employed by meeting attendees and project leads noting empty consensus.

"Our meeting ended in vicious agreement: all nodded, none executed, the perfect loop of nothingness."

Related Terms: Consensus building, Rubber stamp, Groundhog Day

VIEWABILITY

n. A metric determining whether an ad was actually seen by a user. Commonly employed by advertisers, publishers, and marketers improving ad performance.

"We bragged about high viewability, ignoring that viewers scrolled by at light speed, barely registering our existence."

Related Terms: Conversion rate, Programmatic advertising, A/B testing

VILLAGE HALL MEETING

n. A smaller, informal meeting with senior management to discuss issues. Commonly employed by organizations seeking open dialogue but on a smaller scale.

"The village hall meeting promised open dialogue but delivered corporate karaoke of buzzwords."

Related Terms: Town hall, Chime in, Consensus building

VIRAL GROWTH

n. Rapid spread of a product or service as users share it widely. Commonly employed by startups, marketers, and growth hackers seeking explosive adoption.

"We hoped for viral growth, but our product barely got a sniffle's worth of interest."

Related Terms: Growth hacking, User acquisition, A/B testing

VIRAL MARKETING

n. Strategies encouraging customers to share a product, boosting reach exponentially. Commonly employed by marketers, social media teams, and digital advertisers.

"Our viral marketing attempt spread like cold oatmeal—slow, unwelcome, and disappointing."

Related Terms: Viral growth, Influencer marketing, Cross-channel marketing

VISIBILITY TO

n. The level of access or awareness one has regarding a topic or issue. Commonly employed by managers, stakeholders, and analysts wanting clarity.

"We had visibility to the data, which meant squinting at tiny charts and hoping something made sense."

Related Terms: In the loop, Sense check, Context

VISION

n. A bold or ambitious direction or goal an organization aims to achieve. Commonly employed by executives, founders, and branding teams inspiring direction.

"Our vision statement soared so high that practicality fainted at the altitude."

Related Terms: True North, Core values, Visioning

VISIONING

n. A session focusing on future planning and setting strategic directions. Commonly employed by executives, coaches, and consultants encouraging forward thinking.

"Our visioning workshop ended with dreamlike scenarios and zero steps to reach them—magical indeed."

Related Terms: Vision, Marinate, Deep dive

VOLDIS

n. A discount given for purchasing in large quantities or at a reduced price. Commonly employed by buyers, wholesalers, and sales teams.

"We got a voldis on bulk orders, basically paying less to store more things we might never sell."

Related Terms: Freemium, Cost-benefit analysis, Penny wise, pound foolish

VOLUNTEER ENGAGEMENT

n. Recruiting, training, and maintaining relationships with volunteers. Commonly employed by nonprofits, community groups, and event organizers.

"Our volunteer engagement strategy involved free T-shirts and lukewarm 'Thanks for showing up!' emails."

Related Terms: Donor stewardship, Nonprofit sector, Community outreach

VOLUNTOLD

v. Being assigned a task under the guise of volunteering, often without a real choice. Commonly employed humorously by employees, managers, and coworkers.

"I got voluntold to organize the holiday party—my enthusiasm was as authentic as artificial snow."

Related Terms: CYA (Cover Your Ass), Playing politics, Busy work

VUBICLE

n. A cubicle located next to a window, offering better views and natural light. Commonly employed by office planners, employees, and HR discussing workspace perks.

"Upgrading to a vubicle meant enjoying sunlight while ignoring the fact that we're still in a cubicle."

Related Terms: Twobicle, Hot desking, Culture fit

VULTURE CAPITALISTS

n. Investors profiting by buying struggling companies cheaply and selling off assets. Commonly employed by critics, media, and insiders describing predatory behavior.

"The vulture capitalists circled our failing startup, drooling over its final crumbs of value."

Related Terms: VC (Venture Capital), Corporate welfare, Regulatory capture

W

IS FOR WORKFLOW BECAUSE WORKING WISELY WITHIN WELL-DEFINED WORKFLOW WARDS OFF WASTAGE AND WORRY.

W-CUBED (WWW)

n. A playful term for the 'www' in website addresses. Commonly employed jokingly by employees referencing old internet lingo.

"We told clients to check w-cubed dot oursite, feeling very 1997."

Related Terms: Triple-dub, Cloud-based, E-commerce

WAG (WILD-ASSED GUESS)

abbr. + n. A rough estimate made without solid data. Commonly employed humorously by employees, managers, and analysts admitting guesswork.

"Our sales forecast was a WAG, as scientific as picking numbers out of a hat."

Related Terms: Knee-jerk reactions, Cost-benefit analysis, Counterfactual

WIGGLE ROOM

n. Flexibility to make adjustments or changes to terms, deals, or agreements. Commonly employed by negotiators, project leads, and executives allowing leeway.

"We had so little wiggle room that even breathing felt like breaking policy."

Related Terms: Marinate, Table stakes, Circle back

WALK SCORE

n. A measure of how walkable an area is based on proximity to amenities. Commonly employed by real estate agents, urban planners, and homebuyers.

"Our office's walk score was so low, stepping outside required a map, a car, and a prayer."

Related Terms: Zoning laws, Regional development, Community outreach

WALLET SHARE

n. The proportion of a customer's total spending directed to a specific company. Commonly employed by marketers, sales teams, and financial analysts.

"We fought for more wallet share, but customers barely gave us a coin's worth of attention."

Related Terms: Customer journey, Conversion rate, Value proposition

WASTED BANDWIDTH

n. Spending time or resources on activities that don't advance objectives. Commonly employed by employees, managers, and consultants identifying inefficiencies.

"Arguing over logo colors was wasted bandwidth, a scenic detour from doing real work."

Related Terms: Busy work, Donkey work, Flogging a dead horse

WAX POETIC

v. Speaking in an elaborate, flowery way, often excessively. Commonly employed by presenters, executives, and writers indulging in grandiose language.

"Our CEO waxed poetic about 'disruptive paradigms,' while we searched for meaning in the syllables."

Related Terms: Management speak, Fluff, Corporate lingo

WEAPONS GRADE

adj. Extremely effective or potent, so strong it could be dangerous. Commonly employed humorously by coworkers, managers, and observers praising intensity.

"Our coffee was weapons grade—one sip and you saw tomorrow's deadlines in HD."

Related Terms: Wow factor, Value add, Uber

WELLNESS PROGRAMS

n. Employer or insurer-sponsored initiatives promoting healthy lifestyles and preventive care. Commonly employed by HR, benefits managers, and health insurers.

"Our wellness program offered yoga at dawn and kale smoothies, ignoring that we prefer sleep and donuts."

Related Terms: Value-based care, Community outreach, CSR (Corporate social responsibility)

WHEEL SPINNING

v. Putting in effort without making meaningful progress. Commonly employed by employees, managers, and critics noting wasted motion.

"We spent the morning wheel spinning: lots of activity, zero destination, and a squeaky metaphorical tire."

Related Terms: Busy work, Flogging a dead horse, Groundhog Day

WHISTLEBLOWER

n. A person who exposes unethical or illegal behavior within an organization. Commonly employed by regulators, media, and governance bodies encouraging accountability.

"The whistleblower revealed our accounting shortcuts, turning our quiet office into a soap opera overnight."

Related Terms: Whistleblower protection, Government accountability, CYA (Cover Your Ass)

WHISTLEBLOWER PROTECTION

n. Legal safeguards preventing retaliation against individuals reporting misconduct. Commonly employed by lawmakers, NGOs, and compliance officers ensuring safety for informants.

"With whistleblower protection, we hoped truth-tellers wouldn't need to wear disguises in the break room."

Related Terms: Whistleblower, Government accountability, Policy advocacy

WHITE SPACE

n. Unexplored opportunities or gaps in a market not yet capitalized on. Commonly employed by strategists, innovators, and investors.

"Our strategy aimed at white space, though we ended up coloring outside the lines with confusion."

Related Terms: Go-to-market strategy, Disruption, Bubble mentality

WHITEBOARD

n. Using a physical or digital board to brainstorm, visualize, or communicate ideas. Commonly employed by teams, facilitators, and teachers fostering creativity.

"We whiteboarded so many plans that the marker fumes became a mood board of dizziness."

Related Terms: Brain dump, Deep dive, Ideate

WHORE'S MARKET

n. A highly competitive, no-barriers market where anyone can participate easily. Commonly employed very informally or controversially by critics or insiders.

"In this whore's market, everyone peddled something—talent optional, desperation guaranteed."

Related Terms: Cutthroat, Disruption, Red ocean

WIN-WIN

n. A solution or agreement beneficial to all parties. Commonly employed by negotiators, mediators, and leaders seeking mutual gains.

"We promised a win-win, but reality delivered a lose-lose, and we settled for a draw."

Related Terms: Consensus building, Buy-in, Vicious agreement

WINDOW OF OPPORTUNITY

n. A limited time during which certain actions yield optimal results. Commonly employed by managers, strategists, and sales teams timing offers.

"Our window of opportunity closed when the competitor launched their offer first."

Related Terms: Marinate, Circle back, Sense check

WOMB TO TOMB

phrase. Covering the entire lifespan of a product, process, or service from start to finish. Commonly employed by managers, historians, and analysts studying full cycles.

"We managed the product womb to tomb, nurturing it until it died quietly in a dusty server."

Related Terms: Soup to nuts, Business transformation

WORK STREAM

n. A distinct set of tasks or activities within a larger project or initiative. Commonly employed by project managers, program leads, and cross-functional teams.

"We split the launch into two workstreams: building the product and making excuses for delays."

Related Terms: Workstream, Break down silos, Critical path

WORKFLOW

n. The sequence of steps or processes through which work passes from start to finish. Commonly employed by operations managers, IT, and process improvement teams.

"Our workflow resembled a Rube Goldberg machine built by drunk inventors."

Related Terms: Broken workflow, Bottleneck, Lean methodology

WORKSTREAM

n. Another reference to a focused series of tasks contributing to a common goal. Commonly employed by project managers and programs breaking down complex efforts.

"We had multiple workstreams like tributaries flowing into a river of missed deadlines."

Related Terms: Work stream, Scope, Matrices

WOW FACTOR

n. A special element impressing clients or customers. Commonly employed by marketers, product managers, and sales teams wowing audiences.

"We added glitter to the packaging for a wow factor—customers just asked if the product caused a rash."

Related Terms: Value add, Weapons grade, A/B testing

WRAP (ONE'S) HEAD AROUND

phrase. Attempting to understand something complex or difficult. Commonly employed by employees, managers, and learners tackling complicated topics.

"We tried to wrap our heads around the new pricing model and got mental sprains."

Related Terms: Unpack, Deep dive, Sense check

X

IS FOR EXIT STRATEGY BECAUSE EXECUTING AN EXIT ELEGANTLY EXEMPLIFIES EXPERT EXCELLENCE—EXIT WITHOUT EXCUSES!

XAAS (ANYTHING AS A SERVICE)

abbr. A model extending the "as-a-service" concept to virtually anything—software, platforms, infrastructure—monetizing the air you breathe if they could. Commonly employed by tech vendors, cloud providers, and futurists who slap "X" on everything to sound advanced.

"Our XaaS offering included staplers-as-a-service, billed monthly, because why own anything outright?"

Related Terms: SaaS, Freemium, Dynamic pricing

XBRL (EXTENSIBLE BUSINESS REPORTING LANGUAGE)

Abbr. A standard for reporting financial data in a machine-readable format, ensuring accountants can torment spreadsheets in new, thrilling ways. Commonly employed by CFOs, auditors, and analysts craving uniform data formats and alphabet soups.

"We used XBRL so the regulators could read our earnings reports and sigh more efficiently."

Related Terms: Due diligence, Transparency, Regulatory compliance

X-FACTOR

n. That elusive, intangible quality making a person, product, or pitch irresistibly appealing—at least until you realize it's all smoke and mirrors. Commonly employed by HR, branding experts, and execs hoping mystique sells better than logic.

"We hired him for his X-factor, which turned out to be a fancy tie and a louder laugh, nothing more."

Related Terms: Value proposition, Culture fit, Innovation

X-FUNCTIONAL (CROSS-FUNCTIONAL) TEAMS

adj. Teams composed of members from different departments, working together to ensure confusion reigns supreme and blame is universally distributable. Commonly employed by project leads, PMOs, and managers who believe variety fixes everything.

"Our X-functional team combined marketing, finance, and a random intern for 'synergy,' resulting in a masterpiece of mutual incomprehension."

Related Terms: Matrix team, Break down silos, Consensus building

X-SELL (CROSS-SELL)

v. Encouraging customers to buy related or complementary products, as if the initial purchase wasn't enough of a wallet assault. Commonly employed by sales reps, customer success teams, and anyone chasing that sweet upsell.

"We tried to X-sell printer ink to customers buying toothpicks—apparently synergy has its limits."

Related Terms: Upsell, Conversion rate, Customer journey

X-DOCK (CROSS-DOCK)

v. A logistics practice moving products directly from inbound to outbound shipments without warehousing, saving time and sanity—allegedly. Commonly employed by supply chain managers and warehouse gurus who hate forklifts idling.

"We X-docked goods so fast our boxes thought they were speed dating."

Related Terms: Lean methodology, Low-hanging fruit, Optimize

X-CHANNEL (CROSS-CHANNEL)

adj. Involving multiple communication or distribution channels simultaneously, just to ensure customers can ignore you from every platform possible. Commonly employed by marketers, advertisers, and UX designers who believe more paths mean more confusion.

"Our X-channel campaign annoyed people equally via email, SMS, and carrier pigeon."

Related Terms: Cross-device tracking, 360-degree view, Conversion rate

X-INDUSTRY (CROSS-INDUSTRY)

adj. Spanning multiple industries, often touted to justify bizarre partnerships and mind-boggling mergers. Commonly employed by consultants, VCs, and business development leads who think mixing oil and lemonade is genius.

"Our X-industry venture combined fintech and organic farming, yielding invoices as fresh as lettuce."

Related Terms: Bubble mentality, Business transformation, Moonshot Division

X-SHORE (CROSS-SHORE)

adj. Leveraging multiple geographical locations—onshore, offshore, nearshore—in some unholy alliance of time zones and cultural misunderstandings. Commonly employed by outsourcing firms, global PMOs, and managers who love 3 AM conference calls.

"Our X-shore strategy meant someone was always awake, confused, and waiting for an email reply."

Related Terms: Off the record, Under the radar, Hostage mentality

X-MARKET STRATEGY (CROSS-MARKET STRATEGY)

n. A plan targeting multiple market segments at once, spreading resources thinner than cheap margarine on burnt toast. Commonly employed by CMOs, strategists, and execs who believe more markets equals more money—eventually.

"Our X-market strategy chased everyone, catching no one, but looked ambitious on PowerPoint slides."

Related Terms: Go to market, High level, Low-hanging fruit

Y

IS FOR YTD (YEAR TO DATE) BECAUSE YEAR TO DATE YARDSTICKS YIELD YAWNS OR YELPS—YOU'RE YET TO DELIVER, YESSIR!

YEAR-OVER-YEAR (YOY)

abbr. Comparing performance, revenue, or results from one year to the same period the previous year to gauge progress or decline. Commonly employed by analysts, CFOs, and executives evaluating trends without seasonal excuses.

"Our profits soared year-over-year, but somehow we still felt poorer—go figure."

Related Terms: Quarter over quarter, Key Performance Indicator (KPI), High level

YEAR-END CLOSE

n. The financial and administrative process wrapping up all activities at the end of a fiscal year, finalizing records and reports.

Commonly employed by finance teams, auditors, and managers putting a tidy bow on annual chaos.

"During our year-end close, we discovered a stash of unfiled invoices dating back to the Bronze Age."

Related Terms: Fiscal responsibility, Due diligence, Transparency

YEAR-END REVIEW

n. A formal evaluation of annual performance, outcomes, and progress, often used for appraisals, bonuses, or strategic planning. Commonly employed by HR, executives, and employees hoping for praise—or fearing scorn.

"Our year-end review was a marathon of polite nods and forced compliments."

Related Terms: Performance management, Key takeaway, Above my paygrade

YTD (YEAR TO DATE)

abbr. The period between the start of the year and the current date. Commonly employed by accountants, analysts, and managers tracking performance.

"YTD, we achieved 50% of our goals—if our goal was confusion, we hit 110%."

Related Terms: Quarter / Q, EOD/EOW, ROI (Return on Investment)

YEARLY CADENCE

n. A schedule or rhythm set on an annual basis, used for recurring tasks, reports, or product launches. Commonly employed by project managers, planners, and marketing teams timing big announcements.

"Our yearly cadence ensured we panicked about the same deadlines every twelve months."

Related Terms: Quarterly cadence, QBR, High level

YELLOW FLAG

n. A warning sign or potential issue needing attention. Commonly employed by managers, analysts, and team leads noting early concerns.

"A yellow flag popped up when customers asked, 'Is this safe to use?' more than once."

Related Terms: Red tape, CYA (Cover Your Ass), Flag

YELLOW LIGHT

phrase. A cautionary signal in project management or reporting, indicating concerns that are not yet critical but need attention. Commonly employed by team leads, project managers, and PMOs highlighting mild trouble ahead.

"We gave the initiative a yellow light—still rolling, but buckle up for bumps."

Related Terms: Red flag, Broken workflow, Bottleneck

YIELD MANAGEMENT

n. Adjusting prices or allocations of resources based on demand patterns to maximize revenue or efficiency. Commonly employed by airlines, hotels, and pricing analysts exploiting every profitable window.

"Our yield management strategy changed ticket prices so often that even we got dizzy."

Related Terms: Dynamic pricing, Capacity constraints, CPA (Cost Per Acquisition)

YES-MAN

n. An individual who habitually agrees with their superiors or the prevailing opinion, often stifling honest feedback. Commonly employed by managers, cynical coworkers, and boards lamenting lack of innovation.

"Our yes-man nodded at every half-baked idea as if it were divine prophecy."

Related Terms: Stepford Worker, Culture fit, Broken record

YOGA BREAK

n. A short pause in the workday dedicated to stretching, relaxation, or wellness activities, ironically offered to reduce stress from endless meetings. Commonly employed by HR, wellness committees, and cheerful memos pretending work isn't a grind.

"Our yoga break gave us ten minutes of serenity before returning to Slack pings."

Related Terms: Wellness programs, DNB, Clock watcher

YOUNG TURKS

n. Ambitious, energetic younger employees eager to challenge the status quo and push new ideas. Commonly employed by executives and HR noting fresh talent that rattles old norms.

"Our young turks questioned every legacy process, leaving veterans both impressed and annoyed."

Related Terms: Moonshot Division, Disruption, Innovation

YOUR MILEAGE MAY VARY (YMMV)

phrase. An informal disclaimer that results or experiences may differ for each individual, reducing definitive claims. Commonly employed by colleagues, reviewers, and product leads hedging promises.

"'This new tool boosts productivity—YMMV,' said the trainer, basically dodging all accountability."

Related Terms: My understanding, It is what it is, Don't boil the ocean

YARDSTICK

n. A measure or standard used to compare performance, success, or progress. Commonly employed by execs, analysts, and team leads seeking tangible benchmarks.

"We used last quarter's results as a yardstick, discovering we barely measured up."

Related Terms: Benchmarking, Key takeaway, Net-net

Z

IS FOR ZONING LAWS BECAUSE ZAPPING ZANY ZONING REGS ZIPS BUSINESS INTO ZONES— ZERO IN ON ALLOWABLE AMBITIONS AND ZOOM AHEAD!

ZBB (ZERO-BASED BUDGETING)

abbr. A budgeting method starting from zero each period, requiring all expenses to be justified rather than carried over. Commonly employed by CFOs, finance teams, and cost-cutting consultants aiming for lean operations.

"Under ZBB, we explained why we needed pens, and I'm not kidding."

Related Terms: Fiscal responsibility, Cost-benefit analysis, Lean methodology

Z-LISTER

n. A low-priority individual, team, or brand considered the least influential or desirable compared to higher "letter" tiers. Commonly employed by insiders, execs, and critics ranking people or initiatives by importance.

"Our new vendor was a Z-lister nobody heard of, but we signed them anyway—go figure."

Related Terms: Dead weight, Mom-and-pop, Multi-slacker

ZERO-BASED THINKING

n. Approaching decisions as if starting from scratch, ignoring past assumptions or practices. Commonly employed by strategists, innovators, and consultants wiping slates clean to find fresh solutions.

"With zero-based thinking, we axed traditions so old even HR forgot why they existed."

Related Terms: Marinate, Pivot, Disruption

ZERO CYCLES

phrase. Having no available time or capacity to take on more tasks. Commonly employed by overworked employees, managers, and IT staff.

"We had zero cycles left, yet new requests poured in like confetti at a 'Time's Up!' party."

Related Terms: Time-poor, Busy work, ALAP (As Late As Possible)

ZERO DEFECT STRATEGY

n. A quality control approach aiming for no errors or defects, often considered idealistic. Commonly employed by manufacturing lines, product teams, and quality gurus chasing perfection.

"Our zero defect strategy meant weekly panic attacks over a single misplaced comma."

Related Terms: Quality assurance (QA), Lean methodology, Continuous improvement

ZERO FOOTPRINT

adj. Claiming minimal or no impact on resources, space, or environment. Commonly employed by sustainable-minded firms, IT departments (cloud-based solutions), and marketers seeking eco-cred.

"We called our remote server zero footprint, ignoring the giant energy bills."

Related Terms: Carbon pricing, Greenfield site, Philanthropic giving

ZERO LATENCY

adj. Operations or systems with virtually no delay, often idealized in data processing and communication. Commonly employed by IT, data analysts, and service providers promising instantaneous responses.

"Our zero latency dashboard updated so fast we still ignored it—no time for data."

Related Terms: Analytics, Machine learning, Optimize

ZERO-SUM GAME

n. A situation where one party's gain is exactly matched by another's loss. Commonly employed by negotiators, strategists, and economists describing competitive scenarios.

"Our sales battle felt like a zero-sum game: if we win this client, the competitor cries, and vice versa."

Related Terms: Cutthroat, Playing politics, Disruption

ZERO TRUST MODEL

n. A security framework assuming no user or system is inherently trusted, requiring strict verification. Commonly employed by cybersecurity teams, IT admins, and paranoid CIOs.

"Under the zero trust model, even our printer needed a password and a background check."

Related Terms: Regulatory compliance, Due diligence, Offline

ZERO-IN

v. To focus intensely on a specific goal, problem, or target. Commonly employed by managers, project leads, and consultants encouraging sharp focus.

"We zeroed-in on the client's complaints, discovering they hated our font—progress!"

Related Terms: Deep dive, Low-hanging fruit, Move the needle

Z-SCORE

n. A statistical measure indicating how many standard deviations a data point is from the mean, often used in finance or analytics. Commonly employed by quants, analysts, and data-driven teams comparing performance to norms.

"Our Z-score suggested our sales were an outlier—just not the good kind."

Related Terms: Quant jockey, Analytics, Machine learning

ZOMBIE MEETING

n. A meeting that serves no purpose and refuses to end, draining energy. Commonly employed by employees, managers, and team leads mocking pointless gatherings.

"The zombie meeting shuffled on, devouring our will to live one agenda item at a time."

Related Terms: Meeting hell, Bullshit bingo, Vicious agreement

ZOMBIE PROCESS

n. A technical process continuing to run without usefulness or function. Commonly employed by IT, developers, and sysadmins killing pointless background tasks.

"Our app's zombie process haunted the server, chewing up memory like a restless phantom."

Related Terms: Technical debt, Scalability issues, Broken workflow

ZOMBIE PROJECT

n. A project repeatedly revived despite being deemed unsuccessful in the past. Commonly employed by managers, employees, and teams forced to resurrect doomed efforts.

"We resurrected the zombie project again, hoping this time it wouldn't bite our morale."

Related Terms: Sunk cost fallacy, Scope creep, Groundhog Day

ZONE OF POSSIBLE AGREEMENT (ZOPA)

(Noun) The range within which two parties may find common ground to strike a deal in negotiations. Commonly employed by negotiators, dealmakers, and strategists ensuring everyone leaves slightly satisfied.

"We found our ZOPA just before negotiations derailed into polite muttering."

Related Terms: Consensus building, Buy-in, Marinate

ZONING LAWS

n. Local regulations dictating how property can be used (residential, commercial, etc.). Commonly employed by urban planners, developers, and local governments.

"Zoning laws prevented us from building a shooting range on the roof—apparently it's frowned upon."

Related Terms: Public policy, Regional development, Greenfield site

ZOMBIE PIPELINE

n. A sales or project pipeline filled with leads or tasks that never progress, yet aren't removed, haunting reports indefinitely. Commonly employed by sales managers, project leads, and marketers lamenting stale data.

"Our zombie pipeline gave us hope and frustration in equal measure—undead leads never buy."

Related Terms: Churn, Herding cats, Donkey work

HEY LEGEND!

LIKE FREE STUFF? WE'VE GOT YOU COVERED!

We at Cleveland Steamer Press can't thank you enough for picking up this book and making it all the way through. Hopefully, you were able to disrupt a cross-functional synergy or even better, a board meeting with your wit and this book!

As a token of our appreciation, we'd love to give you a free book on us. This one is slightly less SFW! Scan the QR code below to claim yours and keep the good times rolling.

We hope you enjoyed this book and thank you again for supporting independent publishing. If you're interested in our other books, please visit our website: www.clevelandsteamerpress.com

www.ingramcontent.com/pod-product-compliance
Lightning Source LLC
Chambersburg PA
CBHW071528220526
45469CB00003B/679